Bloom's Literary Places

DUBLIN
LONDON
NEW YORK
PARIS
ROME
ST. PETERSBURG

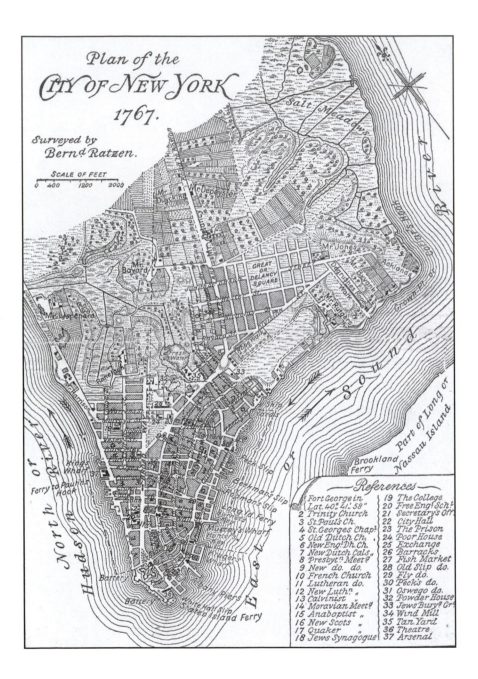

Plan of the
CITY OF NEW YORK
1767.

Surveyed by
Bernd. Ratzen.

SCALE OF FEET
0   400   1200   2000

References

1 Fort George in Lat. 40°. 41'. 59"
2 Trinity Church
3 St. Pauls Ch.
4 St. Georges Chapl.
5 Old Dutch Ch.
6 New Engh. Dh. Ch.
7 New Dutch Cals.
8 Presbytn. Meetg.
9 New do. do.
10 French Church
11 Lutheran do.
12 New Luthn. „
13 Calvinist
14 Moravian Meetg.
15 Anaboptist „
16 New Scots „
17 Quaker „
18 Jews Synagogue
19 The College
20 Free Engl. Schl.
21 Secretary's Off.
22 City Hall
23 The Prison
24 Poor House
25 Exchange
26 Barracks
27 Fish Market
28 Old Slip do.
29 Fly do.
30 Peck's do.
31 Oswego do.
32 Powder House
33 Jews Bury. Grd.
34 Wind Mill
35 Tan Yard
36 Theatre
37 Arsenal

Bloom's Literary Places

NEW YORK

Jesse Zuba

Introduction by
Harold Bloom

CHELSEA HOUSE
PUBLISHERS
A Haights Cross Communications Company
Philadelphia

CHELSEA HOUSE PUBLISHERS
VP, NEW PRODUCT DEVELOPMENT Sally Cheney
DIRECTOR OF PRODUCTION Kim Shinners
CREATIVE MANAGER Takeshi Takahashi
MANUFACTURING MANAGER Diann Grasse

BLOOM'S LITERARY PLACES
EXECUTIVE EDITOR Matt Uhler
SERIES AND COVER DESIGNER Takeshi Takahashi
LAYOUT EJB Publishing Services

A Haights Cross Communications ✦ Company

http://www.chelseahouse.com

First Printing

9 8 7 6 5 4 3 2 1

Library of Congress Cataloging-in-Publication Data

Zuba, Jesse.
    New York / Jesse Zuba ; edited by Harold Bloom.
        p. cm. — (Bloom's literary places)
    Includes bibliographical references and index.
    ISBN 0-7910-7838-8 (alk. paper)
    1. Literary landmarks—New York (State)—New York. 2. American lit-
erature—New York (State)—New York—History and criticism. 3.
Authors, American—Homes and haunts—New York (State)—New York.
4. New York (N.Y.)—Intellectual life. 5. New York (N.Y.)—In literature. I. Bloom, Harold. II. Title. III. Series.
    PS144.N4Z83 2004
    810.9'97471—dc22

ISBN 0-7910-7838-8 (HC) / 0-7810-8358-6 (PB)

TABLE OF CONTENTS

HAROLD **BLOOM**

Cities of the Mind

It could be argued that the ancestral city for the Western literary imagination is neither Athens nor Jerusalem, but ancient Alexandria, where Hellenism and Hebraism fused and were harvested. All Western writers of authentic aesthetic eminence are Alexandrians, whether they know it or not. Proust and Joyce, Flaubert and Goethe, Shakespeare and Dante rather uneasily share in that eclectic heritage. From the mid third century before the Common Era through the mid third century after, Alexandria was the city of the spirit and mind, where Plato and Moses did not reconcile (which would be impossible) but abrasively stimulated a new kind of sensibility, that we have learned to call Modernism, now twenty-six centuries old. The first Modernist was the poet Callimachus, who said that a long poem was a long evil, and together with his colleagues were approvingly named as *neoteroi* (modernists) by Aristarchus, the earliest literary critic to attempt making a secular canon. Dr. Samuel Johnson, Boileau, Sainte-Beuve, Lessing, Coleridge, I.A. Richards, Empson, Kenneth Burke are descendants of Aristarchus.

F.E. Peters, in his lucid *The Harvest of Hellenism*, summarizes

the achievement of Hellenistic Alexandria by an impressive cat-
alog: "Gnosticism, the university, the catechetical school, pastoral poetry, monasticism, the romance, grammar, lexicography,
city planning, theology, canon law, heresy and scholasticism". I
don't know why Peters omitted neo-Platonism, inaugurated by
Plotinius, and I myself already have added literary criticism, and
further would list the library. Alexandria has now exiled its
Greeks, Jews, and mostly everyone else not an Arab, and so it is
no longer the city of the mind, and of the poetic tradition that
went the long span from Callimachus to Cavafy. Yet we cannot
arrive at a true appreciation of literary places unless we begin
with Alexandria. I recommend the novelist E.M. Forster's guide
to the city, which deeply ponders its cultural significance.

We are all Alexandrians, as even Dante was, since he
depended upon Hellenistic Neo-Platonic interpretations of
Homer, whose poetry he had never read. Vergil, Dante's guide,
was Hellenistic in culture, and followed Theocritus in pastoral,
and Alexandrian imitations of Homer in epic. But though our
literary culture remains Alexandrian (consider all our ongoing
myths of Modernism), we follow St. Augustine in seeing
Jerusalem as the City of God, of King David and his martyred
descendant Jesus of Nazareth. Our universities, inescapably
Alexandrian in their pragmatic eclecticism, nevertheless continue to exalt the Athens of Socrates, Plato, and Aristotle as the
city of cognition and of (supposed) democracy. The actual Peri-
clean Athens was a slave-owning oligarchy and plutocracy,
which still prevails in much of the world, be it Saudia Arabia or
many of the Americas. Literary Athens, in its Golden Age, built
on Homer and produced the only Western drama that can challenge Shakespeare: Aeschylus, Euripides, Sophocles and the
divine Aristophanes (I follow Heinrich Heine who observed
that: "There is a God and his name is Aristophanes".)

Athens now slumbers except for Olympic games and
tourism, while Jerusalem is all too lively as the center of Israeli-
Arab contention. Alas, their literary glories have waned, but so
have those of Rome, where Vergil and even the Florentine

Dante are little read or emulated. Cities of the mind are still represented by Paris and London, both perhaps at this moment in cognitive decline. The international language is now American English, and New York City is therefore the literary place-of-places. That, of necessity, has mixed consequences, but those sharpen my renewed comparison to ancient Alexandria, which mingled inventiveness with high decadence, at the end of an age. Alexandria was consciously belated and so are we, despite our paradoxical ecstasy of the new.

2

Is a literary place, by pragmatic definition, a city? Pastoral, like all other literary forms, was an urban invention. The Hebrew Bible, redacted in Babylonian exile, has as its core in Genesis, Exodus, Numbers, the Yahwist's narrative composed at Solomon's highly sophisticated court in Jerusalem. We cannot locate the inception of what became *Iliad* and *Odyssey*, but the Greece they taught centered at Athens and Thebes. Florence exiled Dante and Cavalcanti, yet shared all further vernacular literary development with Rome and Milan. If Montaigne tended to isolate himself from embattled Paris, he knew his readers remained there. Elizabethan-Jacobean literature is virtually all fixated upon London, and centers upon Shakespeare's Globe Theater. If the American Renaissance emanates out of the Concord of Emerson, Thoreau, Hawthorne, it is equally at home in the New York City of Whitman, Melville, and the burgeoning James family. Though Faulkner kept, as much as he could, to Oxford, Mississippi, and Wallace Stevens to Hartford, if I had to nominate the ultimate classic of the United States in the twentieth century, unhesitatingly I would choose the poetry of Hart Crane, Whitman's legitimate heir as the bard of New York City. Kenneth Burke, whenever I saw him from 1975 on, would assure me again that Whitman's "Crossing Brooklyn Ferry" and Hart Crane's *The Bridge* were the two greatest American poems.

Our best living novelists—Philip Roth, Pynchon, DeLillo—

have become inseparable from the ethos of New York City. Only the elusive Cormac McCarthy, seer of *Blood Meridian*, keeps far away from the city-of-cities, which has displaced London and Paris as the world's imaginative capital.

3

However solitary a major writer is by vocation, he or she tends to find a closest friend in a contemporary literary artist. Perhaps rivals attract: Shakespeare and Ben Jonson, Byron and Shelley, Hawthorne and Melville, Hemingway and Scott Fitzgerald, Eliot and Pound, Hart Crane and Allen Tate are just a few pairings, to stay within Anglo-American tradition. Yet the tendency is everywhere: Goethe and Schiller, Wordsworth and Coleridge, Swift and Pope, Tolstoy and Chekhov, Henry James and Edith Wharton, and many more, too numerous to list. The locales waver: Hemingway and Fitzgerald in Paris, Byron and Shelley in Italian exile together, Eliot and Pound in London. There are giant exceptions: Cervantes, Milton, Victor Hugo, Emily Dickinson, Joyce and Beckett (though only after their early association).

Cities are the essential requisite for literary relationships, including those dominated by a father-figure, the London assemblage of the Sons of Ben Jonson: Carew, Lovelace, Herrick, Suckling, Randoph and many more, or Dr. Samuel Johnson and his club of Boswell, Goldsmith, Burke, among others, or Mallarmé and his disciples, including Valéry, who was to surpass his master. Modernist London always calls up Bloomsbury, with Virginia Woolf as its luminous figure, the ornament of a group that in its own idiosyncratic mode saw E.M. Forster as its patriarch.

Even in the age of the computer screen, proximity is essential for literary fellowship. But so far I have considered the city as literary place only in regard to writers. As subject, indeed as *the given* of literature, the city is a larger matter. The movement from garden to city as literary focus is powerfully clear in the Hebrew Bible, when Yahweh moves his abode from Mount

Sinai to Mount Zion, and thus to Solomon's Temple. As the mountain of the Covenant, Sinai stands at the origin, but surprisingly Ezekiel (28:13 following) locates "Eden, the garden of God" as a plateau on Zion, both cosmological mountain and paradise. When Yahweh takes up residence in the Temple, his Eden is close by, yet nevertheless the transition from garden to city has been accomplished. This is the Holy City, but to the literary imagination all the great cities are sacred: Paris, London, Dublin, Petersburg, Rome, and New York are also sanctified, whatever suffering and inequity transpire in them.

4

In the United States the national capital, Washington D.C., is scarcely a city of the mind, not only when contrasted to New York City, but also to Boston, Chicago, San Francisco. Paris, London, Rome are at once capitals and literary centers, but Washington D.C. has harbored few major American writers and has provided subjects only for political novelists, like Henry Adams and Gore Vidal. The Great American Novel perpetually remains to be written, despite such earlier splendors as *The Scarlet Letter*, *Moby-Dick*, *Huckleberry Finn*, and *The Portrait of a Lady*, and a handful of later masterpieces from *As I Lay Dying* and *The Sound and the Fury*, *The Sun Also Rises* and *The Great Gatsby*, on to *Gravity's Rainbow*, *Sabbath's Theater*, *Underworld*, and *Blood Meridian*. I rather doubt that it will take Washington, D.C. as subject, or be composed by an inhabitant thereof.

The industrialization of the great cities in the nineteenth century gave us the novels of Victor Hugo, Dickens, Zola which produced a realism totally phantasmagoric, now probably no longer available to us. Computer urbanism does not seem likely to stimulate imaginative literature. Visual overdetermination overwhelms the inward eye and abandons us to narrative or the formal splendors of poetry and drama. There is something hauntingly elegiac about fresh evocations of literary places, here and now in the early years of the Twenty-first century.

Introduction

The imaginative literature of New York City is superbly ongoing. Its recent splendors include Tony Kushner's double-drama, the epic theater of *Angels in America*, and the luminous later work of John Ashbery, the most eminent living poet of the English language. Don DeLillo's extraordinary *Underworld* and Philip Roth's series of novels that include his masterwork, *Sabbath's Theater*, are a high testimony to the exuberance and vitality of the world's city, even in the aftermath of the destruction of the Twin Towers. Whether you choose to regard the City-of-Cities as Poe's and O. Henry's Babylon on the Hudson, or as the mixed but vibrant vision of the American Dream, the literary magnificence of its celebrants and deplorers seems not likely to wane.

Of all the celebrants, the authentic prophets remain two of our half-dozen greatest poets, Walt Whitman and Hart Crane. The others—Emily Dickinson, Robert Frost, Wallace Stevens and T.S. Eliot—remain identified respectively with Amherst, Vermont, Hartford, and voluntary exile in London. Whitman, born and raised in Long Island, and Hart Crane in Garretsville, Ohio, are more than identified with Manhattan and Brooklyn.

Rather, to a literary sensibility, New York City is now identified with *Song of Myself,* "Crossing Brooklyn Ferry", *White Buildings,* and *The Bridge.* In this brief foreword to Jesse Zuba's superb and poignant book, I will center on "Crossing Brooklyn Ferry" and *The Bridge,* for they embody the mythmaking that haunts the City forever. Stand on the Brooklyn Heights promenade and stare across Brooklyn Bridge to the towers of Manhattan, and you relive the creative ecstasy of the two American poets I continue to find essential to imaginative life.

1

Flood-tide below me! I see you face to face!

Clouds of the west—sun there half an hour high—I see you also face to face.

Crowds of men and women attired in the usual costumes, how curious you are to me!

On the ferry-boats the hundreds and hundreds that cross, returning home, are more curious to me than you suppose,

And you that shall cross from shore to shore years hence are more to me, and more in my meditations, than you might suppose.

2

The impalpable sustenance of me from all things at all hours of the day,

The simple, compact, well-join'd scheme, myself disintegrated, every one disintegrated yet part of the scheme,

The similitudes of the past and those of the future,

The glories strung like beads on my smallest sights and hearings, on the walk in the street and the passage over the river,

The current rushing so swiftly and swimming with me far away.

The others that are to follow me, the ties between me and them,

The certainty of others, the life, love, sight, hearing of others.

Others will enter the gates of the ferry and cross from shore to shore,
Others will watch the run of the flood-tide,
Others will see the shipping of Manhattan north and west, and the heights of Brooklyn to the south and east,
Others will see the islands large and small;
Fifty years hence, others will see them as they cross, the sun half an hour high,
A hundred years hence, or ever so many hundred years hence, others will see them,
Will enjoy the sunset, the pouring-in of the flood-tide, the falling-back to the sea of the ebb-tide.

O harp and altar, of the fury fused,
(How could mere toil align thy choiring strings!)
Terrific threshold of the prophet's pledge,
Prayer of pariah, and the lover's cry, —

Again the traffic lights that skim thy swift
Unfractioned idiom, immaculate sigh of stars,
Beading thy path—condense eternity:
And we have seen night lifted in thine arms.

Under thy shadow by the piers I waited;
Only in darkness is thy shadow clear.
The City's fiery parcels all undone,
Already snow submerges an iron year . . .

O Sleepless as the river under thee,
Vaulting the sea, the prairie's dreaming sod,
Unto us lowliest sometime sweep, descend
And of the curveship lend a myth to God.

Knowing that Brooklyn Bridge had replaced Brooklyn Ferry, Crane extends and intensifies Whitman's vision of New York City as epitome of an America that bridges past and future, Old World and New, the poet's aspiration and his desperation, his wound and his divine hope. Crossing to Manhattan is transformed into the spiritual experience of finding the Unknown God of America, not Mammon nor yet the American Jesus, but something ever more *about to be*, a possible sublimity. At seventy-four, I keep returning to New York City, seeking some sign of what Walt Whitman and Hart Crane hymned. On the surface, it hardly is there to be found, but where else can it be so urgently sought?

CHAPTER ONE

New York Through
the Eyes of Alfred Corn

Alfred Corn, widely acclaimed as a poet and a critic, is the author of *All Roads at Once, A Call in the Midst of the Crowd, Notes from a Child of Paradise, The West Door,* and most recently, *Contradictions.* He currently resides in Rhode Island, but for many years he lived in New York, the appeal of which he had felt from afar while growing up in South Georgia. The city's landscape, history, and atmosphere are beautifully and powerfully evoked in "A Call in the Midst of the Crowd," the *Paterson*-like long poem from which his 1978 collection takes its title. The following conversation took place on August 19, 2003.

Jesse Zuba: There's a poem in your recent book, *Contradictions,* about first coming to New York to stay. Could you elaborate on that moment of arrival—what kinds of preconceptions you might have had, what sort of a first impression the city made on you?

Alfred Corn: Well, let's get the purely external facts down first. I had been an undergraduate in French literature at Emory. My plan in those days was to get a doctorate and teach French at the university level. I chose to go to Columbia because it was in New York, and I'd always harbored a secret ambition to live there, and that had been on my mind from an early age. You have to imagine someone growing up, interested in the arts, in South Georgia in the 50s: there wasn't that much to do or see. Basically what came to me was through books and television and movies. And somehow the image of New York City just always had a special aura. It was the capital of America, at least culturally. I might not have viewed it this way at the time, but later on it seemed to me that looking back, New York was also the capital of the 20th century ... certainly by the 20s. Now you could say that there are several world capitals that cooperatively hold that distinction, but for most of the 20th century that honor went to New York.

So I showed up to begin my graduate studies, and the immediate problem was to find a place to live. I didn't have a lot of money—I had some scholarship assistance, but nothing else, and I decided not to take on the extra work so I could focus on my classes. There wasn't much I could afford. I ended up staying up in one room of an apartment owned by a very old lady who had lived in Morningside Heights for probably 40 years. This was in 1965. She gave me a room for 10 dollars a week. You wouldn't quite call it a tenement. The building wasn't bad really, but her apartment was seldom cleaned and she was just too old to take care of it. There wouldn't have been many takers for that room—that's why it was so cheap.

I had been to New York only once before, for one night, on my way to France, in the summer of '64. So my only preparation for moving there was that one visit, along with what I had seen in movies and read in books ... not really an adequate preparation. It was an overwhelming experience to arrive there, and look about, and see things that I had only heard about or seen images of. Suddenly I was *in* those images.

I remember that the noise level was a lot to get accustomed to. It was a twenty-four hour city then, as it still is, and the noise just never stopped. I had a window out onto Amsterdam

Avenue where there was a lot of traffic: it took me a long time to get adjusted.

JZ: Did you know anyone who could show you the ropes?

AC: I had no friends in New York, no one except an English professor who'd just moved there from Emory, where I got my undergraduate degree, and his wife, who was at NYU—like me a French major. Apart from those two people I knew no one. I had an uncle who worked at the Museum of Natural History, but I never saw him because he lived in New Jersey.

I had to start learning the city from scratch. It was like beginning life all over again, and this time I had the freedom to invent myself. I remember liking the anonymity, because if you grow up in a small town in South Georgia, you know everyone and everybody knows who you are, who you hang around with, what your business is. In New York nobody knew me, so I didn't have to deal with anyone's preconceptions about me. That gave me a kind of heady sense of freedom. The other thing that struck me was that, you know, southerners have an exaggerated politeness, and, well, New Yorkers don't. I reveled in the freedom not to be "nice."

JZ: You mentioned you had an idea of New York before you went there. Is there anything you can remember, specifically, that inspired you to live in New York?

AC: Well, there were movies like *On the Waterfront*, *Marty*, *West Side Story*, and *Asphalt Jungle*, which presented the city as a bit dangerous, but fascinating. They weren't necessarily exalted things, but I found TV shows like *I Love Lucy* very funny, and there were talk shows or game shows like *What's My Line* that featured wisecracking New Yorkers. The panelists had a witty, ironic approach to things. In the same vein was the movie *All About Eve*. I thought it would be wonderful to attend a smart theatrical party where everyone was drinking martinis and saying smart, brittle things to each other. I wanted to be able to talk like that.

JZ: Was the city you imagined the city you found?

AC: I led two lives there: I led the life of a graduate student, which was fairly ordinary. Columbia, you know, because it's an Ivy League school, has always been *in* New York but not quite *of* it. So it did seem a separate world. The city itself of course is anarchic by nature and thus quite different. One thing that I was looking forward to: I'd recently let myself realize that I was gay, and I thought that gay life would be much freer in the city. I think that it probably *was* the freest place for a gay person in America at that time. Which didn't mean it was utterly free. It wasn't common to be out as a gay man. A professor spoke to me once about meeting Richard Howard, the poet, and how surprising it was that Richard was perfectly candid about being gay. That was presented as a strange anomaly. It's kind of hard nowadays to imagine, but that's how it was. I'm not sure how I found them, but I did go down to the Village and discover several gay hang-outs. The most famous one still exists—Julius's, probably the oldest gay bar in Manhattan.

I have to say I was a little disappointed: it wasn't that easy or comfortable for me to make my way as a gay person in New York. Partly because of inexperience. And partly the repressive atmosphere: back then bars were still being raided by the police. I don't think they tended to take people in, but they might look at their ID's and clear the bar. So there was some trepidation to cross the threshold into certain places. I remember that I was discouraged by the difficulty of finding someone to be with long-term. There were casual connections, but exclusive partnering seemed to be outside everyone's gameplan. As an antidote to loneliness, I began to make friends, I guess mostly with fellow graduate students. But no long-term relationships. And I think that's actually part of the city's spirit—to function on one's own, to be one little atom in its swirling environment. It's a very strange feeling, certainly it made a strong contrast with my own upbringing. Suddenly you were a single speck, with no permanent connections, and with millions of other specks around you.

JZ: That sense of New York seems pretty central to "A Call in the Midst of the Crowd," even its title. Had you been writing poems before then? Or did you start writing after you arrived in the city?

AC: Like most high school students I wrote poems, but that had more to do with being an adolescent than being a poet. I think my ambitions had shifted to novel-writing by the time I was a graduate student. One thing that happened about a year after arriving in New York was that I met Edmund White, who hadn't been published yet at the time but is now quite famous. And that's what I hoped would happen in those years: that besides being a graduate student I would meet writers and artists. And slowly that began to happen. I'd say it accelerated a bit once I had met Edmund because he's a gregarious person, meets people easily; and through him I got to know other writers, for example, Richard Howard, whose reputation, as I said, preceded him. It was Richard who introduced me to the critic David Kalstone. Later on, David became a kind of mentor. Before we became close, I was writing fiction—actually, Edmund and I used to read each other chapters from our developing novels.

Can we backtrack a bit? I mentioned that before enrolling at Columbia I'd gone to a language program in Avignon. While there in France I'd met a woman named Ann Jones, who had been at NYU and was about to transfer to Berkeley. We kept in touch after that summer by letters, in one of which I explained that I was gay. The news didn't ruffle her. In fact, the year after I came to Columbia she came to Columbia as a grad student in Comp Lit, and we began to live together. The long-term relationship I had been looking for I suddenly had, and surprisingly it was with a woman. The occasion of Ed's and my first meeting was a party that a gay friend of mine gave down in the Village, and Ann of course came with me. I think that part of the interest that I had for him was that I was a gay man, she knew it, and that was perfectly okay with her. He found that really unusual and fascinating, wanted to know about me, about us, and so we became friends.

He had written a novel about a young gay man coming to New York and working for Time Life books. Ed had done the same thing after getting his undergraduate degree at Michigan. I read it and said it was good, but in those years I was focused on avant-garde writing, the *nouveau roman,* and so forth. Well, I told Ed I thought his novel was well done, and I enjoyed reading it, but that it could have been written in the 19th century. That he had to bring himself up-to-date, do something a little more experimental. He was rather annoyed with me, I think, legitimately. Shortly after that he began working on a new novel. He would bring chapters of it and read them to Ann and I, and it was clear he was really onto something, something new and unusual. It wasn't a *nouveau roman,* more the genre of the fantastic. Because of the encouragement Ann and I had given him, when he published it, his first novel, he dedicated it to us. It's called *Forgetting Elena,* and in many ways it's his most original novel.

JZ: A lot of what you've been talking about resonates with a passage by Frank O'Hara which you quote in "A Call in the Midst of the Crowd": "John Ashbery, Barbara Guest, Kenneth Koch and I, being poets, divided our time between the literary bar, the San Remo, and the artists' bar, the Cedar Tavern. In the San Remo we argued and gossiped: in the Cedar we often wrote poems while listening to the painters argue and gossip. So far as I know nobody painted in the San Remo while they listened to the writers argue." I wonder if you could say some more about what kind of impact being close to people like Edmund White, David Kalstone, Richard Howard, perhaps your professors or fellow grad students at Columbia, had on you and your writing.

AC: It's a subject I've thought about a lot. I sometimes ask myself what if that night I'd had the flu and I hadn't ended up going to that party and didn't meet Ed. Starting out as a writer is a lonely prospect. Writers sort of provide warmth and light for each other, they encourage each other, and early on writers tend to overestimate the value of their friends' work. That's very important, actually, because there are so many obstacles to be overcome, you need all the encouragement you can get. So Edmund and I began to supply some of that for each other, and he introduced me to David Kalstone, who seemed impressed by my ability to write. He made suggestions about what to read, and so did Richard Howard. Meeting poets like Richard, or people who were interested in poetry like David, my ambitions at the time had begun to shift back toward being a poet. Eventually through David I met John Ashbery and James Merrill. I think it was a little bit intentional on his part: he knew that if I was going to make my way I'd have to have a little boost here and there. For example James Merrill used to come to New York and stay at David's, and David artfully placed my poems around the apartment, which Merrill then read and asked, "Who is this?" That led to a meeting with him at David's apartment on West 22nd Street, which led in turn to a correspondence with him. He became something of an advisor. It often happens that way, a kind of chain reaction.

Another thing I should say is that, growing up in the South I knew some Jewish families, but not many. One exciting thing about New York was that there were so many Jews there. David was Jewish, and Richard as well. The culture of the Jewish intellectual became very important to me. I remember that Edmund and I read Susan Sontag's *Against Interpretation*, and exchanged ideas about those essays. The intensity and passion of Jewish writers became very important to me. I set myself the project of learning as much as I could, and appropriating as much as I could.

JZ: What happened after you left the grad program?

AC: It gradually dawned on me that I was in the wrong career track. It was the late 60s, there was turbulence everywhere, and an anti-institutional bias across the board. I began to question whether I could ever fit the mold that would be required—a responsible, dutiful professor of French at a university. One of the clichés of that era was, "Turn on, tune in, and drop out." I dropped out. I was a hippie for a while; I took drugs. It seemed impossible to envision for myself a middle-class life as a professor. It was spring of 1970 when I made the decision not to pursue my degree.

So without any prospects I quit the program and tried to make my living as I could. I remember my first job was for a publication called *University Review*—a tabloid-format newspaper aimed at graduate students and undergraduates, which was given out free. I had to do everything: I stuffed envelopes, wrote articles, conducted interviews with various notables—A. J. Ayer, Jack Nicholson, Bernardo Bertolucci—whatever needed doing. I remember delivering several thousand newspapers once. It was a nutty job, but it got my feet wet. After that I had a series of odd jobs. I was a sort of factotum at a cultural center on the Upper West Side. My expenses were few.

By then the marriage had ended—a mutual decision made by Ann and me. I found another long-term relationship, with a man this time, a beginning architect. He was one of the pioneers to move to SoHo, which had just opened up as a residential area for artists. He and his friends bought a building down on Grand and Mercer and began converting it into living lofts. When we moved in, it was just raw space with one water tap feeding a bath-tub, nothing else. It was not the SoHo of today, but instead small industries, storage, warehouses, and so forth. There were no grocery stores or laundries. There was one restaurant, called Food, and one bar called Fanelli's. There were a few other artists living around, but otherwise it was just an industrial area, and about as noisy a place as you could imagine. There were trucks roaring by at all hours of the night. Urban bohemia. When we moved in, there were about two inches of dust on the floor, and we gradually made a living space out of it.

JZ: How long did you live there?

AC: We got there in the spring of '72; he and I parted company about four years later. I moved out temporarily to Brooklyn, Columbia Heights. I'm sure you can guess why.

JZ: There's a poem in your first book about going out and trying to visit Hart Crane's home, and settling instead for reading his "To Brooklyn Bridge" on Brooklyn Bridge, because his building wasn't there any more. I wonder if, with Crane in mind—as well as Whitman, Stevens, Merrill, Ashbery—all of whom seem to have influenced your poetry, all of whom lived in New York at one time or another—you could talk about what it's like to try to live in a place so crowded with the presence of your heroes.

AC: It was very important to me. Just the fact of residing in New York seemed to be a kind of endorsement. The streets of New York were hallowed by the fact that Whitman and Crane had trudged along them. Not incidentally for me, they both were gay. I know some people don't think that Whitman was, but to me that's nonsense. Harold Bloom talks about the anxiety of influence, and I remember writing to him once, in a letter, saying that I don't think that when gay writers deal with gay precursors the anxiety is as intense as it is for straight writers. Let's say that you are a beginning poet, straight, male, and you begin to write poetry because you've read something else: that's going to produce a certain anxiety. Somehow or other that anxiety is tempered when both you and the precursor are gay because, apart from being some sort of literary "parent," your precursor could, on the imaginary plane, have been a partner. Which involves a different set of psychological reflexes.

JZ: So that made New York a place that you could draw energy from ...

AC: That's right. I felt that being in New York, the home of so many writers, helped to endorse my own project. Figures like Whitman or Crane, after all, weren't well integrated into any social or literary establishment. If they, with those disadvantages, had managed to succeed, then perhaps I could too, and on the same turf. With Crane the similarities are really quite striking: he came from elsewhere, a long way elsewhere, like me, and then worked at a series of odd jobs. Even with those disadvantages, he became a key American poet for the first part of the century. So that helped reassure me that I wasn't totally deluded in my ambition to try to do something similar.

JZ: Who among poets, or among novelists, film-makers, playwrights, musicians, painters, really conveys the atmosphere of the city the way it felt to you?

AC: F. Scott Fitzgerald has some extraordinary passages about New York, and Henry James. When you come to poetry, you certainly get a good coverage of Harlem in the work of Langston Hughes. Which brings me to another observation: I think that some of the most compelling portraits of life in New York are in music, especially jazz. I think jazz captures the sound of the city better than prose or poetry. My own special favorites are Charlie Parker, John Coltrane, Miles Davis, and Billie Holiday, but there are really so many great jazz artists. Mondrian has a painting which I think he must've made after he'd come to New York called "Broadway Boogie Woogie." The title by itself shows a jazz influence. And then there's this pulsing grid, which could be an abstract visual equivalent of jazz syncopation, or else it's the grid of Manhattan streets with the traffic lights flashing. Or both.

JZ: There's a poem in your first book about an exhibit at the Met Museum of Chinese porcelains. With poems like that in mind, poems that find their occasion in the city, on a street or in a museum, in "real life" or art, it seems that an advantage of living in New York, particularly for an artist, is the sheer abundance and availability of subject matter in so many different forms.

AC: Some people dislike art about art. But I don't. It's not a hang-up for me. I like primary subject matter, too. Think about some of the New York painters—they look outside the window, paint what they see, and suddenly there it is on the wall. The various arts feed into and off of one another. The 50s was one of the great periods of New York art: you had great jazz musicians playing, Abstract Expressionist painting, in particular, De Kooning and Pollock, and of course poets. You could see a synergy developing among them. Now, to some degree I think that has continued, but I'm not sure it's as powerful as it was.

JZ: That kind of synergy is interesting—the idea that artists working in different mediums are bound to grow, somehow, because of proximity to one another. But it seems difficult to define precisely how that network of relationships brings that about. Is there a way to get more concrete about what that synergy really is?

AC: Well, we've already talked about the endorsement that living in a place in which art has been made, is being made, confers. Then I think you're influenced unconsciously by the physical fact of the city in ways that you don't even know. And there are artworks that you see, that have a connection to the city as subject matter, so that you say to yourself, "I'd like to do something like that." The opportunities for something like that to occur are increased in a place like New York.

JZ: In "A Call in the Midst of the Crowd," you quote a passage from a letter by Wallace Stevens, written when he was living in Manhattan, in which he talks about going up on his roof and gazing at the Wanamaker's sign across the way. It's interesting to think about what kind of affect New York had on a writer like Stevens, who was there only temporarily. Could you comment on Stevens's time in New York? Do you think it was important to him?

AC: It must have been. I suppose he could have practiced law in other places, but he chose New York, so he must have had some kind of yearning to be there. Then he moved to Hartford, which, interestingly enough, was a kind of outpost of the avant-garde in the 20s and 30s. But Stevens definitely kept in touch with people in New York and visited from time to time because he was interested in developments in the art world. He was interested in European art and European life, certainly, but he felt that as an American he should write about America, so he produces poems like "An Ordinary Evening in New Haven." Somehow to be an American was to be less conventionally Romantic, and that notion is manifest in his poetry, though the word "Wanamaker" never appears.

JZ: This touches on New York's ties to Europe and its cities. I wonder if you could hold forth on the idea of New York as a kind of European city that happens to be located in America.

AC: It's literally the easiest point of departure to Europe and vice versa. Traditionally, New York was a primary destination for Europeans visiting the United States. And of course New York had mass migration of Jews who were leaving Europe during the Nazi era, many of whom became culturally prominent. Those refugees brought with them knowledge and expertise, sophistication. So it is the most Europeanized city in America. There are foreign language bookstores. The Met Museum contains art from every part of the world, every era. Theater is imported from England. In my day, there was a lot of interest in French cinema in New York: a month or two after a film came out in Paris it would appear in New York with subtitles.

JZ: In what ways does New York differ from European cities?

AC: Let's start with the most obvious—the visual aspect. Now more cities are beginning to resemble New York, but as late as the 60s, no other city had that spectacular series of high rise buildings, made possible by the bedrock that underlies most of Manhattan. It also has an unprecedented population density, at least compared to the capital cities of Europe. You're going to have crowded conditions on the streets and in the subway. It's not a comfortable, easy city to live in, and it never has been. You read the diarists of the 19th century and they complain about the same things—crowding, noise, rubbish everywhere. The same complaints echo through the centuries.

On the other hand, it has always seemed to me a capital of freedom in a way that the European capitals are not. The French, for all that they have espoused in avant-garde art, remain socially rather decorous. There's a restraint. And of course the English have always been known for that, at least until the past decade. But New York always had an aura of freedom, not to say lawlessness.

It has a strange beauty—and a strange ugliness entirely different from what you see in other cities. Things that used to be truly unbearable, like the elevated, have been gotten rid of. A loud train shrieking past would never have been allowed in a European city. But in New York, monetary considerations, natural considerations, have sometimes made the city extremely ugly, so it's different in that respect. And there's the unusual democracy of the crowds—the very rich live among the very poor—certainly they jostle each other, rub elbows, in the streets. Everybody mingles with everybody, unless they make a really strong effort not to. It's so cosmopolitan; every national group has its little enclave. So if you want to have Cambodian cuisine, you can find it. And if you want to find Nigerian artwork, you can find it.

JZ: You spoke about the inconveniences of living there, the challenge of living in New York. There are some lines from the beginning of "A Call in the Midst of the Crowd": "Sheer perversity I guess makes me plumb/the mirror of this self-imposed city/for what, if anything here, holds a promise." And then the

Hart Crane-esque lines: "The speaking gift that falls to one who hears/a word shine through the white noise of the world." The idea of the city being self-imposed, like a discipline, or a challenge, interested me. Could you talk about the value of meeting that challenge?

AC: Well, I wasn't born there. When you live in New York, you meet more people who have come there from somewhere else than you do native New Yorkers. I didn't have to be there; I chose it. And because of the difficulty and inconvenience, residing in Gotham is a discipline. You have to give up so much to make a go of it. But there's a value that you receive from doing so. And that was what I assumed, that there was such a value.

Also, New York has been the site of a great deal of suffering. The poverty evident in the Jacob Riis photographs, for instance. New York history has chapters of terrible violence. I thought that part of the appeal too had to do with this more negative aspect. The Japanese filmmaker Kurosawa says somewhere that the artist does not "avert his eyes." I somehow felt that, in order to qualify as an artist in the 20th century, I had to confront the worst. And so the negative aspect of the city interested me. Some of the worst angst I've ever experienced took place in New York. It can seem enormously alienating—frightening, cold, indifferent, like its skyline, as though the city itself somehow had a being that was distinct from that of its inhabitants. I felt that to have an art that failed to take that into account was to have a limited art. I wanted to have the negative as well as the positive.

Also I felt, as Crane did, that there was a visionary aspect to the city. Something unprecedented in the aspirations of its builders. I wanted to get at that as well. It is extraordinary how much energy has been brought to bear on those few square miles. It's a cliché that there's "a broken heart for every light on Broadway." So many people poured their energies into the city, saw it as something larger than themselves, and it didn't always return the compliment. I wanted to see if I could discern what that singular appeal was, what made New York a site of aspiration, in spite of all the obstacles.

JZ: What did you find?

AC: Some of the physical artifacts there, like the Brooklyn Bridge, seem to embody the ideal version of the city that many of its inhabitants had in mind. If you look at a poem like Crane's "Atlantis," there's a kind of upward aspiration, a propulsion into the future, an abandonment of all that was easy in order to go into uncharted territory.

JZ: In "A Call in the Midst of the Crowd" you say that it's a "small wonder that I belong here/with difficulty." With Crane, who was not a native New Yorker, in mind, I wonder if you could talk about how important it was to you to "belong" to the city, or if there's some kind of advantage in feeling like an outsider, confronting its "difficulty" deliberately, like a discipline.

AC: I didn't feel that I belonged very much to the milieu that I grew up in. I felt proud to be a New Yorker, partly because it was so difficult. But I didn't feel adequate at first: there was so much remedial work to do in order to catch up. It took me several years before I even felt qualified to describe myself as a New Yorker.

JZ: What kind of work did that involve?

AC: New York has the most difficult subway system in the world. And I can remember back to when I wasn't familiar with it. I don't think in those years that they even had the maps that there are now that show the routes of the trains. So I took long trips. Just finding your way around was a big part of that work. But I also didn't feel as though I knew enough—not just about the city, but about everything. So I made it my business to acquire the body of information that a respectable, intellectually inclined New Yorker should have. That meant reading lots of books and seeing movies and going to plays, as well as spending a lot of time walking around the different neighborhoods. I had as a project at one time to visit every block in Manhattan. Of course I never succeeded. I lived at 14 different addresses during my time in New York. I always made a point of exploring in every direction when I came to live somewhere new. Unlike most New Yorkers, I actually became a dedicated guidebook tourist in New York. I went to see the lesser-known sites, such as the Jumel mansion in Washington Heights, which figures in Gore Vidal's novel *Burr*.

JZ: Where else?

AC: I very much recommend the Hispanic Society's museum. They have works by Velasquez, Goya, El Greco. No one ever goes there, but it's things like that that I would search out. There's the Poe Cottage in the Bronx where Edgar Allen Poe lived. There's the Cloisters. There's any number of things. And of course all the obvious things, too—Ellis Island, the Statue of Liberty, the Empire State Building ... The native New Yorker tends not to be interested even in the big attractions. Many native New Yorkers have never been to Ellis Island. They grew up there, and so they take it all for granted.

JZ: Your poem registers the idea that there's so much going on in New York with the idea of the city's "hum." This idea comes up in many of the excerpts you quote as well. James mentions "the welter of objects and sounds," and Crane talks about the "chaos" of the city. Crane also describes in a letter the group of people he's dined out with recently, but then he goes on to say in the same excerpt that, paradoxically, he's never felt more solitary. Could you say something about the possibility that New York naturally positions you, native or non-native, both, "in the game and out of the game," to use Whitman's phrasing? "We all but believed something untoward might happen," you say at one point in your poem, "not just mischief ... but a true celebration,/and that O for once we might feel/that all of us belong in the same space,/ company"—which sounds like Crane's "visionary company of love"—"instead of crowding." Could you reflect on the way New York presents you with these options—intense solitude, crowding, and company?

AC: The poem was written in the late 70s about the mid-70s. That was one of the low points in New York history. You're too young to remember. Public services were poor. The activism of the 60s had carried over into the 70s, and you really saw a variety of competing interest groups. A lot of people pulling in a lot of different directions. One of the things said about the recent blackout was that there was almost no looting. The city has become more cohesive. But at that time the naked reality of competing interest groups was very apparent. And there wasn't a communitarian spirit so far as I could see. That led to daily conflicts like those in the movie *Taxi Driver*. And that's the context in which that poem was written. We also have to say that, as experience shows, art comes out of conflict.

It was a useful social laboratory in that given the apparent realities of distinctly different interests pulling in different directions, could they even so override self-interest to a degree and cooperate enough to make the city work? It seemed to me that that was possible. And I think that in fact it has proved true—these days it seems like residents will cooperate to a degree.

This is grandiose, but I also think there are lessons to be drawn from the way these intensely competing interest groups eventually scaled self-interest down a bit, I mean, if we take a global perspective and consider competing nationalities. That the world at large could somehow learn from New Yorkers' experiences. That it's possible to act for your nation, your country, and yet cooperate for the sake of the planet where we all have to live. True, the present Administration hasn't taken note, to judge by Mr. Bush's refusal to sign the Kyoto Accords or to heed resolutions passed by the U.N. But maybe things will change.

CHAPTER TWO

Lenape, Dutch, British, American

The explorers, travelers, and missionaries who were the first Europeans to visit the lower Hudson Valley reckoned it a veritable Eden. The land was fertile, and the rivers, lakes, and coastal waters were so rich with fish that they could be caught by hand. The twenty thousand or so Lenape Indians who called the area home when Europeans first arrived only enhanced the ecosystem: animals and vegetation flourished all the more as a result of their planting, burning, and hunting practices. Early visitors' stories and reports suggest the dimensions of the region's abundance. It was possible to catch a 6-foot lobster in the harbor waters and to take a 40-pound wild turkey in the woods. One hunter allegedly killed 11 16-pound geese with a single shot (Burrows and Wallace 4).

Before the Lenapes, bands of nomads lived in the region. They had come in the wake of retreating polar caps that had once placed much of modern New York City under a slab of ice one thousand feet thick. The area's first human inhabitants departed with the big game they hunted as continuing warming transformed the environment. The Lenapes came to the valley nearly seven thousand years ago; they hunted, fished, and raised crops, dotting the area with camps and webbing it with trails. Europeans were struck both by the apparent healthiness of the Lenape people and the ease of their lifestyle: food, water, and materials for shelter and fire were plentiful, so there was little cause for dispute among neighboring clans. But the simplicity of their living arrangements and want of opportunistic regard for the resources that surrounded them were construed by enterprising Europeans as signs of a devilish laziness and inferiority. The commercial promise that the region's riches represented to explorers was to prove the doom of its native occupants.

GIOVANNI DA VERRAZZANO

It was with such promise in view that Giovanni da Verrazzano, a Florentine seaman, piloted *La Dauphine* across the Atlantic in 1524. He had been commissioned to find a route to the Indies by a group of French silk merchants. Instead, in April 1524 he found the Upper Bay, which he mistook for a large lake and named Santa Margarita, in honor of the sister of King Francis I. A storm forced the ship to depart, and Verrazzano continued his search for China and Japan along the Canadian coastline. Esteban Gomez, a Portuguese pilot who had sailed under Magellan, made a similar journey a year later, questing up the Hudson in hopes of reaching the Far East. Verrazzano and Gomez were succeeded by increasing numbers of visitors, including fishermen and trappers. The region is known to have been raided for slaves by the English and Spanish toward the turn of the century, but it was the rapid growth of the fur trade whose consequences were to prove destructive for the Lenape culture as a whole. Initially indifferent to the rewards—blankets, tools, guns, alcohol—that meeting Europe's huge demand for furs presented, European goods gradually found a place in Lenape culture, but not without disrupting its economic and social balances. Lengthy trapping expeditions lured Lenape hunters away, leaving food supplies diminished. Territorial disputes, made especially deadly by newly acquired firearms, arose as clans began to take an interest in claiming areas rich in furs. Furthermore, dependence on liquor sapped the vigor of community life and the authority of leaders.

HENRY HUDSON

It wasn't the promise of animal pelts that drew Henry Hudson in September of 1609 up the river that now bears his name. Like Verrazzano and Gomez, the Englishman had skippered his ship, a Dutch carrack called the *Half Moon*, to American shores in hopes of discovering a northwest passage to China and Japan for the Dutch East India Company. The impression the land and people made on him tempered his disappointment. In "The Third Voyage of Master Henry Hudson," a day-to-day account of Hudson's coastal travels and one of the first pieces of writing set in the area that would become New York City, Robert Juet (an officer on the *Half Moon*) notes both how fine the harbor is and how eager for trade the natives are: "Then wee

The Mad Men of Gotham

It was Washington Irving who gave the city the nickname "Gotham" in the Salmagundi papers in the early 1800s. The name is still used centuries later, but why "Gotham"? Irving's reasons for using it, and Manhattanites' reasons for accepting it, have to do with traditions of popular jokes and folk stories about the original Gotham, a town in England.

The idea of Gotham that Irving, who was out to poke fun at the social mores of upper class New Yorkers, had in mind was one derived from tall tales in which Gotham figured as a village of fools. The tales originated during the Middle Ages; in the mid-1500s they appeared in print under the title *Merie Tales of the mad men of Gotam*. The stories offer fairly light entertainment; in one a Gotham man ties his purse to a hare, which he hopes will enable him to pay his rent on time, but the hare

Anchored, and saw that it was very good Harbour for all windes, and rode all night. The people of the Countrey came aboord of us, making shew of love, and gave us Tabacco and Indian Wheat, and departed for that night; but we durst not trust them" (Jameson 20). Hudson was hoping to find a trade route to the Far East, but as he traveled farther up what he called the "North River," he decided that Asia wasn't getting close enough fast enough and turned back.

Merchants took a particular interest in Hudson's news of lively trading in furs with the tribes along the river and continued to send ships to the area throughout the decade of 1610. The map Captain Adriaen Block brought back with him to Amsterdam in 1614 showed "New Netherland" encompassing lands between the Delaware and Connecticut rivers, including present-day Manhattan, which was designated as "Mannhates." Eager to outdo and undo the Spanish, with whom they competed commercially around the globe, in 1621 the Dutch

runs off with his money. Many of the tales merely portray the simplemindedness of the townsfolk, but some—and here perhaps is the reason Irving's New York didn't reject the nickname right away—cast their folly differently, as a kind of in-joke of their own. In one story from this alternate tradition, the villagers, fearing loss of their lands, refused to allow King John, who declared any ground his foot touched during his travels a public highway, to enter Gotham. When the king sent soldiers to punish them for insubordination, the Gothamites feigned idiocy in various forms: "pouring water into a bottomless tub; painting green apples red; trying to drown an eel in a pool of water ... fencing in a cuckoo" (Burrows and Wallace xiv). The soldiers reported that the villagers were mad, and King John spared them. It was perhaps this more flattering portrayal of Gothamite trickiness that allowed the name to stick.

formed the West India Company, which oversaw and financed the growth of New Netherland. By 1625 voyages led by Cornelis May and Willem Verhulst had brought families of colonists to Manhattan. The following year, Fort Amsterdam was built on the southern tip of the island to protect the company's interests, but not before Peter Minuit, the Director of New Netherlands, completed the fabled purchase of Manhattan from the Lenape for sixty guilders (about 650 current U.S. dollars) in trade goods. It's regularly retold as an even better bargain, with the Lenape receiving a scant 24 dollars for the island. That's the figure an historian writing in 1846 calculated using mid-19th century exchange rates; it has persisted in most versions of the story ever since. In *Gotham*, Edwin Burrows and Mike Wallace cleverly refer to the 24 dollars story as the "Primal Deal"—the kernel of a myth of origins that speaks to a range of interests and anxieties, from confirming New Yorkers' reputation for smart business deals, to heralding the legitimacy of a city founded upon fair trade rather than imperial violence. As Burrows and Wallace suggest, however, the Dutch were soon to prove quite capable of violence. It was probably their interest in reducing the risk of Lenape aggression that prompted them to strike the deal—really a small step in the complex process of securing their hold on a lucrative trading post (xv).

NEW AMSTERDAM

Life in New Amsterdam was anything but refined. As one crooked director replaced another, the quality of food and shelter remained unspeakably poor. Peter Minuit was replaced by Wouter van Twiller, the 27-year-old nephew of Kiliaen van Rensselaer, who was the owner of a 700,000 acre riverside "patroonship." (The term refers to lands the company would grant investors who helped colonize New Netherland by recruiting and transporting settlers across the Atlantic). Van Twiller saw to the construction of New Amsterdam's first church, and attempted, unsuccessfully, to seal off the border between New Netherland and the rapidly expanding British colonies to the north by establishing a trading post on the Connecticut River. Under van Twiller New Amsterdam began to spread across the East River into present-day Brooklyn, primarily as a result of his eagerness to snatch up land by taking advantage of the dubious patroonship program. A well-connected drinker and schemer, van Twiller was replaced in 1638 by Willem Kieft, another well-connected drinker and schemer, whose advantages over van Twiller—he was older, wrote his letters in Latin, was an accomplished water-colorist—did little to help him improve on van Twiller's performance in office.

The 400 or so inhabitants of New Amsterdam that Kieft attempted to govern comprised an unruly band of artisans, soldiers, and speculators from a remarkable array of backgrounds. Just over half of the inhabitants were Dutch; among the rest were English, Swedish, Danish, German, and Irish settlers, as well as a number of African slaves. There were nearly 100 buildings in the town, a fourth of which were taverns and liquor stores. Kieft complained in his reports about the mischief the settlers' taste for booze promoted, but his scruples didn't run deep enough to deter him from setting up a distillery on Staten Island, the first in New Netherland. The garrison at Fort Amsterdam kept the bars well patronized. Their reputation for drinking, fighting, stealing, and engaging the services of prostitutes speaks for the carnivalesque atmosphere that must have prevailed over the city. Kieft's first moves in office reflect the problems he must have encountered: he made new rules against adultery, mutiny, harboring fugitives from neighboring colonies, and stopping work early, among others. The loosening of company control over purchasing land and trading with Indians allowed the city to grow under Kieft. In the 1630s and 1640s settlers set up farms on western Long Island, north of the town in present-day Harlem and across the Hudson in what is now Jersey City.

But Kieft proved inept at maintaining friendly relations with the Indians, from whom he repeatedly attempted to exact tribute and on whom he tried to bring a heavy-handed justice.

The result was a full-fledged war replete with massacres and torture on both sides. One particularly horrific exchange had its origins in the Wiechquaesgeck tribe's refusal to hand over the murderer of a Dutch settler. The tribe was later attacked by members of the Mahican tribe and, forced to seek Dutch protection, made camp near New Amsterdam. Kieft took advantage of their proximity and ordered a surprise attack—a brutal action that culminated with a public display of over 80 Indians' heads in New Amsterdam and a celebratory speech from the director himself. Local tribes responded by banding together and attacking outlying farmsteads, killing whole families and burning up every trace of habitation. The West India Company decided to remove Kieft from office in 1645, but massive damages had already been done, leaving the colony in shambles.

PETER STUYVESANT

His replacement was Peter Stuyvesant, who, still in his 30s, was already a peg-legged company hero with a catalogue of unimpeachable credentials. Educated at the University of Franeker, he had been a company agent since 1630, when he was put in charge of Noronha, an island off the coast of Brazil. Subsequently he was made governor of Curacao, Aruba, and Bonaire in the Caribbean, and led company forces in laying siege to the Spanish at St. Martin, during which he sustained the injury (the work of a Spanish cannonball) that necessitated his wooden leg. He arrived to find the colony little more than an outpost, with most of the settlers having withdrawn in fear of Indian attacks to the area surrounding what remained of Fort Amsterdam, which Stuyvesant compared to a "molehill" overrun by men and livestock. The wretchedness of New Netherlands spurred Stuyvesant's resolve: "I shall govern you as a father his children," he declared to the settlers (Burrows and Wallace 43).

Stuyvesant went about improving New Amsterdam with dogged industriousness. Even a short list of the changes he enacted are impressive, especially in light of the failed efforts of his predecessors. He appointed surveyors to plan and build regular streets and established speed limits. He impounded free-roaming pigs, goats, and cows and forbade disposing of trash and waste in the streets, setting up several official dumps for garbage. Wooden chimneys were prohibited, as well as thatched roofs, to help prevent fires. In 1658, he oversaw the building of New Amsterdam's first hospital. He had an orphanage set up, and saw to it that the city's Reformed Church opened an almshouse for the poor. The same year he organized a police force; it was no NYPD that kept watch over the town through the dark frontier nights, but the force—eight men and a captain who sounded alerts manually using rattles—betokened the earnestness of the new governor's intentions. He personally oversaw transactions in the real estate market, in order to organize what had previously been a chaos of makeshift arrangements and corruption, and he kept retail markets under control by making laws about who could sell what, and where and when they could sell it. Not all of the changes Stuyvesant made in New Amsterdam were guided by humanitarian impulses; rejuvenating the economy and ensuring the growth of the colony were his highest priorities. It was with those goals in mind that he encouraged the importation of slaves to New Netherland. Slaves augmented the work force, expedited the resettling of farms outside of town, and increased the manpower that could be called upon in the event of attack.

With the addition of slaves, the population of the colony nearly quintupled during the first decade of Stuyvesant's rule. With the population growth came the emergence of social classes. The highest of these was comprised mainly of merchants with political connections who did their best to ape Stuyvesant's rich lifestyle. The middle class consisted mostly of craftsmen, tavern keepers, hospital workers, and clerks in various lines of business, while the lower class was occupied by African slaves (Burrows and Wallace 53–56). It was among New Amsterdam's wealthy social elite that the first evidence of a literary culture in the city began to appear. Jonas Bronck (from whom the Bronx derives its name) boasted a library that included 20 books in print, 18 pamphlets, and 17 books in manuscript. What was likely the city's first poem was composed by Jacob Steendam, who after a career with the West India Company went to New Netherland and set up as a farmer and slave trader. Entitled "Complaint of New Amsterdam to her Mother," the poem registers its "Complaint" in couplets uttered by the personified city itself, and portrays its namesake in Holland as a negligent "Mother" who has left the fledgling city "forlorn":

> See! two streams my garden bind,
> From the East and North they wind,—
> Rivers pouring in the sea,
> Rich in fish, beyond degree.
>
> Milk and butter; fruits to eat
> No one can enumerate;
> Ev'ry vegetable known;
> Grain the best that e'er was grown.
>
> All the blessings man e'er knew
> Here does our Great Giver strew,
> (And a climate ne'er more pure)
> But for me,—yet immature,
>
> Fraught with danger; for the Swine
> Trample down these crops of mine;
> Up-root, too, my choicest land;
> Still and dumb, the while, I stand,
>
> In the hope, my mother's arm
> Will protect me from the harm. (Murphy 43)

Steendam delivers a miniature panegyric, counting up the city's many "blessings" in the hope of attracting Dutch military support, since New Amsterdam is still too "immature" to keep the encroaching British colonies to the north—allegorized in the image of the trampling "Swine"—at bay for much longer.

It is questionable whether the ills New Amsterdam suffered were attributable, as Steendam's poem suggests, to the negligence of its "Mother," old Amsterdam, or to the overbearing attention its self-professed "father," Stuyvesant, was lavishing on it. New Amsterdam had grown under Stuyvesant, but its growth brought new problems in turn. Bans, prohibitions, and orders of all kinds flowed from his pen as he tried to keep control over a population increasingly diverse with regard to religious and national affiliations. He quarreled with the Lutherans, tried to expel the Jews, and instated a fine for harboring Quakers. Too, as Steendam suggests in his "Complaint," English villages were springing up on Long Island, and the Swedish settlements to the south and west, in present-day New Jersey and Pennsylvania, were expanding. The colony's growth was ensuring that it would become a concern in the eyes of an ever greater number of interest groups, with the English royalty—who were bent on achieving the international commercial control the Dutch enjoyed—at the top of the list.

NEW YORK

The transfer of New York from the Dutch to the English was accomplished with less drama than Steendam's dark image of the land-uprooting swine had suggested. The Stuarts were restored to the English throne in 1660; James, younger brother of King Charles II and duke of York, was made proprietor of the area stretching from what is now New Jersey into present-day Connecticut. He sent Colonel Richard Nicolls and a sizable armed force to take control of New Amsterdam. With the colony on the verge of total disarray, Fort Amsterdam undermanned and understocked, and many of the city's citizens sympathetic to the idea of a change of leadership, Stuyvesant gave up. The terms the English offered were pretty generous anyway: everyone was guaranteed life, liberty, and property so long as they surrendered peacefully. On September 8, 1664, Nicolls officially took control of the city and the region surrounding it. The biggest immediate changes were nominal: Fort Amsterdam became Fort James; Fort Orange farther north; Hudson became Albany; and New Amsterdam and New Netherland took the name both have carried since New York.

"A Brief Description of New York," written by Daniel Denton, was the first published account in English of the colony most recently added to the growing British empire. Like Steendam's poem, the aim of Denton's tract, which appeared in 1670, was to advertise the virtues of life in the colony to the people back home. In an introductory letter to the reader, Denton claims to "deal impartially" with his subject, and to describe "nothing" but what he has been "an eye-witness to," yet such is his zeal to lure immigrants across the Atlantic that he disingenuously mentions unconfirmed rumors of precious stones and metals in the very next sentence: "... the natives tell us of Glittering Stones, Diamonds and Pearl ... and the Dutch hath boasted of Gold and Silver ... yet I shall not feed your expectation with any thing of that nature but leave it till a better discovery shall make way for such a relation" (Denton 2). The essay that follows the letter leaves the prospective immigrant with little reason to stay put. Long Island's "Christal streams" run swift and clean; the "Woods and Fields" are so crowded with "delightful flowers, not only pleasing to the eye, but smell, that you may behold nature contending with Art, and striving to equal, if not excel many Gardens in *England*"; "Nature" has been so "prodigal" in supplying the region with "wilde Beasts and Fowle" that anyone with a suitable weapon "may furnish his house with excellent fat Venison, Turkies, Geese, Heath-Hens, Cranes, Swans, Ducks, Pidgeons and the like" (5). Concerning the natives the would-be colonist has little to fear, according to Denton, mostly because by then there weren't many left. Their disappearance he chalks up to divine intervention: there are "few upon the Island and those few no ways hurtful but rather serviceable to the *English*, and it is to be admired how strangely they have decreast by the Hand of God since the English first settling of these parts ... it has been generally observed that where the English come to settle, a Divine Hand makes way for them, by removing or cutting off the *Indians*, either by wars one with the other, or by some raging mortal disease" (6). Above all, New York is a place of opportunity for those "of an inferior rank"—the members of the lower classes back in England likeliest to be predisposed to a change of scenery: "I may say and say truly that if there be any terrestrial happiness to be had by people of all ranks, especially of an inferior rank, it must certainly be here: here any one may furnish himself with land, and live rent-free, yea, with such a quantity of land, that he may weary himself in the walking over his fields of Corn" (14). Though more recent writers are perhaps less likely to brag about rent levels and plentiful land than Denton was, his hyperbolic claims for the city's promise and democratic character, as well as his special emphasis on the opportunities it afforded for economic advancement, echo throughout the literature of New York.

The colony's new administration was as eager as Denton to promote New York's growth and prosperity. The Articles of Capitulation, drawn up just prior to the city's surrender to James, provided in particular for the freedom and safety of Dutch residents. They wouldn't have to leave, they could keep their slaves, religion, and social customs. It was, after all, in the interest of the English that the town's economy stay on its feet, and many of the region's wealthiest residents were Dutch. So it was that Nicolls allowed the Van Rensselaers to keep their massive patroonship and became good friends with the city's ex-governor Stuyvesant, who lived on a large country estate outside of town. Nicolls was called back to England in 1668 and replaced by Colonel Francis Lovelace, who followed suit by cultivating ties with the wealthy Dutch landowners. He even founded a social club, comprised of ten Dutch members and six English, to help strengthen these ties.

NEW YORK TO NEW ORANGE AND BACK AGAIN

It was the working-class Dutch—the small business proprietors who weren't invited to drink punch with Lovelace at the club—whose interests were ignored as rule changed hands. Having been given no voice in political affairs and made to submit to a legal code loaded with clauses for fees and taxes they hadn't agreed to, it's no wonder they welcomed the arrival of the Dutch squadron under Admiral Cornelis Evertsen that brought the city back under Dutch control between the summer of 1673 and winter of 1674. The result of renewed hostility between England and the Netherlands across the Atlantic, the second coming of Dutch rule to New York—renamed New Orange by Evertsen in honor of Prince William—was short-lived. Seven months after Evertsen had forced the city's surrender, Charles II of England agreed to peace with the States-General in terms that provided for the return of territories the Dutch had conquered in the meantime. Major Edmund Andros was named the new governor, and he ran things in much the same way Lovelace and Nicolls had before him, maintaining solid connections with New York's Dutch businessmen, with whom he strategized to achieve James' primary goal—to grow the city's economy.

Andros's ties to the New York Dutch were so strong, in fact, that they became the occasion of his removal from office. He was replaced in 1683 by Colonel Thomas Dongan, an Irish landlord whose Catholicism held an appeal for James, who had recently become a Catholic. Dongan instituted the election of a representative government—the first in the city's history. He drafted the Charter of Liberties and Privileges, which allowed for religious freedom and trial by a jury and mandated that there be no taxation without representation. He also divided the colony up into counties called New York, Kings, Queens, Richmond, and Suffolk. Good relations with the land-owning Dutch were reaffirmed: Dongan doled out land grants of several hundred thousand acres to some of them and vested them with all sorts of lordly powers. He modestly gave himself a 25,000 acre slice of Staten Island which encompassed present-day Dongan Hills.

THE LEISLER REBELLION

Rising religio-political tensions in England led to the extraordinarily complicated events that sparked the Leisler Rebellion. With the death of Charles II in 1685, James became king. He created the Dominion of New England, which incorporated all of the colonies between Maine and New Jersey. Ex-governor Andros returned to New York three years later as the new governor of all of New England; he fired Dongan and appointed Colonel Francis Nicholson the new governor of the colony. However, James II abdicated the throne that summer under pressure from the Parliament, which had persuaded James's Protestant daughter Mary and her husband the Dutch Prince William of Orange to accept the crown. The surprising news reached New York in all sorts of untrustworthy forms, and rumors of plots and counterplots circulated throughout the city. Governor Nicholson refused to recognize the ascension of William and Mary. Members of the militia rallied around charismatic Captain Jacob Leisler and together with a crowd of civilians stormed into the streets, hoping that by ousting Nicholson they would be preventing a papist rising rumored to involve ex-governor Dongan, the town's Irish Catholics and French Huguenots, and even the Iroquois. The rebellion was successful and a makeshift committee appointed Leisler the commander-in-chief of the province.

Leisler's leadership of the city proved brief. He relied on oppressive political action—haphazard arrests and confiscations, harsh taxes—to maintain control, and was finally undone by the wealthy merchants whose interests Leisler had attempted to oppose by overturning the trade laws that favored their enterprises. In 1690 they finally persuaded King William to get rid of Leisler; Colonel Henry Sloughter was named his replacement. Leisler only turned over control of the city when Sloughter arrived in person in the city and showed him the royal commission. Leisler was executed on May 16, 1691, in a public hanging that took place in what is currently City Hall Park.

Because of Leisler's rebellion, New York society broke into a chaos of interest groups, and the governors over the next 30 years—Colonel Benjamin Fletcher, Richard Coote (the earl of Bellomont), Edward Hyde (Viscount Cornbury), Robert Hunter—came and went largely as a result of an intricate political calculus involving the fortunes of England in its wars against France, Whig and Tory interests, the opposition between New York's landowning elite and its rich merchants, and New York's various religious congregations. Beneath the turmoil, the city continued to grow as it always had—rapidly and unsteadily and regardless of who was in charge. The turn of the century saw the opening of the first printshop, revitalized and improved mail service, the first coffeehouse, and the erection of a new City Hall on the corner of Wall and Broad streets. The city's economy during the 1690s and early 1700s was much helped by piracy, which flourished under each governor in turn. Often financed by rich New Yorkers like Frederick Philipse, Nicholas Bayard, and Stephanus Van Cortlandt, privately owned vessels sanctioned by the British Navy to prey on French ships plied the seas on both sides of the globe. Wealthy investors capitalized on the opportunities for illegal trade that New York's pirates afforded them, and small business owners made out too as crew members spent their share of the booty in taverns and shops. As a result, brick houses began to crowd what little space was left to build on in lower Manhattan, more streets were paved with cobblestones, and the city's upper class indulged its taste for exotic finery of all kinds—fancy mirrors, teak furniture, Turkish carpets, ivory fans.

THE EARLY 18TH CENTURY

In the early decades of the 18th century, the city's prosperity continued unchecked, mostly because of its place in the rapidly developing market for sugar. Formerly a luxury, by the 1710s sugar had become a staple of middle-class life in Britain. "White gold," as it was called, was grown in the West Indies on massive plantations, the owners of which relied in turn on New England agriculture for food, which was shipped down to the islands by way of New York. The economic boom spurred growth on every front. Investors relied on a growing pool of bankers and lawyers to insure and document their transactions; sailors flooded the city and patronized its shops; the number of physicians increased as mariners returned to town suffering from all manner of tropical diseases. The population of the city swelled as immigrants from Germany, Ireland, and Scotland voyaged across the Atlantic, often as indentured servants, looking to share in the wealth.

The number of slaves in the city also burgeoned due to the city's new ties to the Caribbean and its riches: nearly half of the households in the city owned a slave in 1712, and nearly a fifth of the city's total population was African American. The labor slaves provided was enormously valuable to the city, but having more slaves in town increased the threat of revolt in the eyes of the administrators. A slave code adopted in 1702 had stripped blacks of most of the rights—to own property and bear arms, for example—the Dutch had allowed them. Now no more than three slaves could congregate at one time in public, they weren't permitted out after dark, and they were no longer allowed to convert to Christianity as a way of securing extra privileges. Owners were allowed powers to punish slaves however they saw fit, and a "Common Whipper" was appointed to whip slaves guilty of public misconduct. Largely as a result of these changes, New York experienced its first slave rebellion in 1712, when two dozen slaves armed with stolen weapons set a building on fire and attacked those who came to put it out. Governor Hunter sent the fort's garrison after them, but they escaped into the woods. When they were found the following day, they were charged with murder and hanged, although several were tortured to death in the cruelest ways the court could devise: one was roasted over a fire for hours until he died, another hung up in chains until he died of exposure or starvation, and another smashed to death, bone by bone, with a crowbar, while chained to a wheel in front of City Hall (Burrows and Wallace 146–49).

FREEDOM OF THE PRESS AND THE SEEDS OF REVOLUTION

The testing of authority in the name of freedom, along with the display of authority in the name of tradition, was the see-saw pattern that many episodes in New York's history seem to have been modeled on in the decades leading up to the Revolutionary War. To look at one notable example: the First Amendment right to freedom of the press had its basis in a legal case involving New York's second newspaper, John Peter Zenger's *Weekly Journal*. (The first was William Bradford's *Weekly Gazette*, which began appearing on November 1, 1725.) Founded in November of 1733 as a vehicle for political opinions opposed to those of Governor William Cosby, New York's latest corrupt leader, the paper ran satire after satire on Cosby and his sidemen until November of the following year, when he ordered that copies of the paper be destroyed and that Zenger be arrested for libel. Having set bail inordinately high, Cosby went so far as to have Chief Justice James Delancy disbar the lawyers who were preparing to defend Zenger. When the trial finally began in the summer of 1735, Delancy continued his efforts on Cosby's behalf, informing the jury that the accuracy of the reports in the *Weekly Journal* wasn't as important to the case as the fact that the governor's authority had been undermined. The jury proceeded, however, to ignore Delancy and acquit Zenger, inspired perhaps by the words of Zenger's lawyer Andrew Hamilton: "It is not the cause of a poor printer nor of New York alone which you are now trying ... No! It is the best cause; it is the cause of liberty" (qtd. in Lankevich 35).

The Treaty of Paris, signed in 1763, ended Britain's long wars with France. Parliament sought to consolidate its newly won control of transatlantic trade, attempting to bring its colonies to heel by levying new taxes, different groups of which came into effect under the Sugar Act of 1764, the Stamp Act of 1765, and the Townshend Acts of 1767. The "cause of liberty" Hamilton had spoken of at the Zenger trial grew into a cause of note in New York, typically enough, because of the negative effects the new acts had on the economic life of the city. The

Sons of Liberty formed in Manhattan in 1765 in response to the Stamp Act and succeeded in organizing resistance to the new taxes on playing cards, newspapers, and other everyday commodities; the act was repealed in 1766. City merchants boycotted British goods throughout the 1760s and early 1770s to protest taxes they hadn't had a voice in deciding upon, which resulted in more parliamentary concessions and repeals. The Tea Act of 1773 ignited the city's anger once and for all. The Sons of Liberty rallied the merchants to yet another boycott and staged a massive protest that sent the tea ship *Nancy* back on its way without unloading in New York's harbor. On April 22, 1774 New York followed Boston's lead in putting on a "tea party" of its own, dumping 18 crates of tea into the bay. New York merchants, urged on by a 19-year-old student at King's College (founded in 1754, now Columbia University) named Alexander Hamilton, called for a Continental Congress, which convened in Philadelphia in September of 1774. Hoping to appeal to New York's notoriously strong commercial spirit, Parliament proposed exempting the city from trade restrictions in 1775, but by that time, the first battles had been fought with the British in Massachusetts, and Manhattan's radical "Committee of One Hundred" was already in control of the city and busily mustering up a militia.

THE REVOLUTIONARY WAR

New York was the scene of a great deal of military action early in the Revolutionary War, as General George Washington led an American army against a huge British force under Lord William Howe in a series of battles for control of the best harbor in the colonies. Revolutionary sentiment in the city peaked early: Washington had the newly drafted Declaration of Independence read aloud on the Commons on July 9, 1776, as a mob pulled down a statue of George III, reusing the metal to cast bullets for Washington's soldiers. Howe moved his army from Staten Island to Brooklyn later that summer, however, and New York's fortunes as a revolutionary city went downhill from there. Outnumbered and out gunned, the Americans were defeated in August at the Battle of Long Island, though Washington was able to stave off total surrender by leading the remnants of his army across the East River in an escape. Howe initiated the Battle of Manhattan in September with a withering bombardment from his naval forces and easily drove the colonial army out of the city and into the hills on the northern part of the island. Washington's troops fought Howe's to a draw in the Battle of Harlem Heights in mid-September, but were forced to retreat still further as Howe advanced, and suffered defeats at the battles of Throgs Neck and White Plains in October. A fire the same year burned to the ground nearly a quarter of the city's buildings, and a second fire in 1778 took out an additional hundred or so houses and shops. New York was the headquarters of the British military for seven years, and its resources were plundered as a consequence. City residents were required to tip their hats to red-coat officers and British cavalry patrolled the streets, where prostitution and espionage were among the only trades to flourish.

Relief from British occupation did not arrive until November 25, 1783, more than two years after Charles Cornwallis had surrendered to Washington at Yorktown. The final act of the revolution took place in New York, as Washington and Governor George Clinton paraded into the city and the British forces withdrew to Staten Island. The city had lost two thirds of its population, including hundreds of Tory merchants who had relocated to Canada to continue as royal subjects; its commercial vigor was sapped; its social and political infrastructure was in ruins. And yet, almost miraculously, it would take only a few decades for the city to recover and take its place at the heart of the life of the newly fledged United States of America.

CHAPTER THREE

Paradise and Inferno

As if the city had cautiously waited until American independence was secure to allow its first professional man of letters to come into being, Washington Irving was born in the spring of 1783, just as the British surrendered at Yorktown. The New York Irving grew up in was entering a decade of rehabilitation made necessary by the ravages of the British occupation. The city brimmed with problems—its government was in disarray, its commercial routines upset, its population depleted and cultural development thrown off track. But the city also shared in the optimism of the newly created nation, and hummed with the potential energy it would need to surmount the obstacles it faced.

As when the British had taken over the city from the Dutch in 1664, the switch from British to American hands after the war occasioned a series of renamings. Queen became Cedar Street, King became Pine Street, and Crown became Liberty Street; King's College became Columbia. In spite of its problems, New York was also named as the location for the capital of the new nation. City Hall on Wall Street was remodeled by Major Pierre L'Enfant into a space that would serve the needs both of the national congress and the state legislature, since New York City was also named the state capital. Washington was unanimously chosen to be America's first president, and on April 30, 1789, he was inaugurated in the newly renovated Federal Hall. Though Philadelphia took over as the national capital just over a year later, New York's coffers and infrastructure had already benefited from its time as the political nerve center of America. Still, some were disappointed by the transfer. Abigail Adams is alleged to have said of Philadelphia that "when all is done, it will not be Broadway" (qtd. in Lankevich 53).

It was the city's merchants that recognized the advantages of a strong central government for the purpose of rejuvenating New York's economy, and it was their know-how and ingenuity that would ensure the city's full recovery. They founded the Society of Merchants and Tradesmen in 1786 to help coordinate the interests of the city's major businesses. In the late 1780s and early 1790s the city's brokers had been gathering under the branches of a buttonwood tree on Wall Street to buy and sell securities. In 1792 they drew up the "Buttonwood Agreement," a contract that organized them into an official association. This self-regulating body was a forerunner of the stock exchange, which was formed just twenty-five years later. Due to the Revolution, New York had lost its primary markets—the West Indies and Canada. Until negotiations with Britain would reopen them, the city's ambitious merchants turned elsewhere. The *Empress of China*, the first ship to carry American goods to the Far East, left the harbor in March of 1784. Regrowth continued in the first decade of the 19th century, largely as a result of wars between France and Britain, which spurred the rise of the country's merchant marine. By 1807 the value of New York's exports had risen beyond that of every other state or city in the union.

Because of the political influence of New Yorkers like Alexander Hamilton, who served Washington as Secretary of the Treasury, and John Jay, who served as Chief Justice, New York was a staunchly Federalist city, controlled by a merchant aristocracy, for the first decade or so after the Revolutionary War. Those leanings changed early in the 19th century owing to the influence of an institution that was to dominate the city's political scene for over a century, Tammany Hall. Inspired by the Society of Cincinnati, a charitable association started by wealthy officers who'd served under Washington, an upholsterer named William Mooney started the Society of St. Tammany, whose membership was originally limited to common soldiers. Dedicated to charity and the cause of liberty, the society met for the first time on May 13, 1788, in a New York City tavern; by 1789 the organization had members in 13 states.

TAMMANY HALL AND AARON BURR

The character of the society's activities was changed decisively in the 1790s, however, by a young lawyer named Aaron Burr, who saw in its ties to the interests of the working classes a chance for himself to rise politically as the voice of the common people. Burr's allies infiltrated the society and called attention to the plight of the lower and middle classes, arguing that no single charitable act would serve the advancement of liberty and democracy so much as a large-scale movement to widen suffrage among the lower echelons of society. In league with fellow Republicans like Thomas Jefferson of Virginia and George Clinton, New York's governor, Burr sponsored the Manhattan Company, which supplied lower Manhattan with fresh water piped in from the Bronx. More importantly for the purposes of the Republican coalition, the company's charter allowed it to invest surplus wealth, a clause that allowed for the creation of the Bank of Manhattan Company. Stocked with Burr's Tammany friends, the bank's board granted mortgage loans right and left, swelling the ranks of working class voters by enabling them to buy property. In 1800 Jefferson was elected president, and Burr vice president, largely as a result of Tammany's disruption of Federalist control over who could vote. Burr lasted only one term in office: he fled after shooting and killing Hamilton on July 11, 1804, in a duel prompted by their repeated political clashes. His legacy to New York was the enormously powerful political machine, Tammany Hall, whose emergence he had almost single-handedly engineered.

WASHINGTON IRVING

The increasing complexity of New York's political scene made for the city's rise as the news capital of the United States. Nearly 100,000 people inhabited New York in 1807, and there were almost two dozen newspapers in print—each with its own political slant and core group of readers. Among them was a peculiar new paper that featured an eclectic mix of political commentary and social satire called *Salmagundi*, started by James Kirk Paulding along with Peter Irving and his brother Washington, who was to become America's first major writer, and, perhaps not coincidentally, the first writer to treat life in New York City as subject matter adequate to the purposes of literature. Named after the first United States president, who reportedly gave the young Irving a pat on the head as he strolled down a Manhattan street, Washington was born on April 3, 1783, the 11th child of Sarah and William Irving, a deacon in the Episcopal Church. The Irvings lived at 128 William Street, where Washington spent much of his youth. He was tutored privately until, at 14, he began at the seminary of Josiah Henderson. But young Irving wasn't a stellar student, and it was outside of class, at operas and plays, that his most genuine interests developed. He eventually took a law degree, but at 20 his literary career had already begun, as his first contributions to his brother's Burrite *Morning Chronicle* started to appear; he signed them "Jonathan Oldstyle, Gent."—a nom de plume that signaled aesthetic affiliations with the Augustan wits of the previous century and a bourgeois social disposition.

It was in the *Salmagundi* papers, however, that Irving's characteristic voice began to emerge. *Salmagundi* presented "The Whim-Whams and Opinions of Launcelot Langstaff, Esq. & Others"—the "others" were "Will Wizard," who handled the theatrical criticism, and "Anthony Evergreen," who specialized in fashion and social life—in occasional essays modeled on those of Joseph Addison and Richard Steele's hugely popular *Spectator* in England. The constant shifting of political alliances in the city afforded the "Knickerbocker" writers of *Salmagundi* ample opportunities to "instruct the young, reform the old, correct the town and castigate the age," as they defined their purposes in the paper's first number (Irving 49). *Salmagundi* appeared irregularly, depending on the speed with which Irving and his confreres could generate material. Its message tended to be haphazard too: one month it is Robert Fulton, inventor of the steamboat and the torpedo, who is caricatured; next month it is *The Town*, a rival periodical, that is parodied; in another instance, it's the city of Philadelphia, New York's rival, which is made fun of. In "The Stranger in Philadelphia," a native New Yorker journeys to Philadelphia, comes to feel homesick for New York because of the lone crooked street in William Penn's perfectly planned city, and then reflects that "Philadelphia is a place of great trade and commerce—not but that it would have been much more so, that is had it been built on the site of New York: but as New York has engrossed its present situation, I think Philadelphia must be content to stand where it does at present—at any rate it is not Philadelphia's fault nor is it any concern of mine, so I shall not make myself uneasy about the affair" (199). It was in this kind of glib, ironic assertion that New York first heard a voice that was both distinctively literary, in light of its connections to British writing, and yet uniquely its own. Fittingly, it was in the 17th issue of *Salmagundi* that the city was given one of its most enduring nicknames: Gotham.

Irving continued to cultivate the genial ironic tone of *Salmagundi* in *A History of New York, from the Beginning of the World to the End of the Dutch Dynasty, by Diedrich Knickerbocker*, which was published in 1809. As the teasingly ambitious title suggests, Irving was setting out to make of New York's history a mock-epic of the origins of America. The book blends accurate historical narrative with gossip and legend, filling in gaps in the record with stories and anecdotes of Irving's own invention.

Much of the pseudo-history of the book works to poke fun at Irving's contemporaries: so it is that figures like Van Twiller, Kieft, and Stuyvesant, New Netherland's actual governors, are implicated in a political milieu drawn from Irving's turn-of-the-century New York. In one well-known passage Irving pits Henry Ten Broek, who was on the board of the Free School in 1807, against William Hardenbroek, who was assistant alderman of the ninth ward of the city in 1809, in the "first altercation on record among the new settlers" concerning the "plan ... on which the encreasing town should be built." Mynheer Hardenbroek, whom Irving calls "Tough Breeches," wants a city intersected "by means of canals ... after the manner of the most admired cities in Holland," while Mynheer Ten Broek, whom Irving refers to as "Ten Breeches," wants to focus on adding space to the city by "run[ning] out docks and wharves." But Tough Breeches will hear nothing of the kind:

> "For what," said he, "is a town without canals?—it is like a body without veins and arteries, and must perish for want of free circulation of the vital fluid." Ten Breeches, on the contrary, retorted with a sarcasm upon his antagonist, who was somewhat of an arid, dry-boned habit of body: he remarked that as to the circulation of the blood being necessary to existence, Mynheer Tough Breeches was a living contradiction to his own assertion; for every body knew there had not a drop of blood circulated through his wind-dried carcase for good ten years, and yet there was not a greater busy-body in the whole colony. (450–51)

Of course, the argument ends inconclusively, so that Irving's taunting of the local big shots is incorporated into a larger joke about the endlessness and inconsequence of political bickering in general. Light as such entertainment might seem, as Knickerbocker quips earlier in *History*, "cities *of themselves*, and in fact empires *of themselves*, are nothing without an historian," even, apparently, if that historian is a mock-pedantic joker (379). By writing New York's present into its past, however whimsically, Irving was conferring upon the city a sense of itself as an important work in progress—a sense the city has cherished to this day. Irving's *History of New York* was the first book by an American to receive praise abroad: Sir Walter Scott, Charles Dickens, and Samuel Coleridge were among those to express enthusiastic approval. Irving had put New York, and America, on the world's literary map.

NEW YORK IN THE EARLY 19TH CENTURY

New York in the 1810s and 1820s was at a turning point in its gradual rise to cultural dominance: the slow recovery from the British occupation was almost complete, and the cultural life of the city was picking up thanks to continued social and economic improvement. On the anniversary of the nation's independence in 1817 New York Governor DeWitt Clinton broke ground for the digging of the Erie Canal, which was completed in 1825 and positioned the city as the middleman between the agricultural and trapping industries of the upper Midwest and European markets. The abolition of the Council of Appointment, which controlled residents' power to vote, increased suffrage, and in turn further empowered the working classes. Slavery was abolished state-wide in 1827 as the result of a bill signed ten years earlier by Governor Daniel Tompkins. The Erie Canal brought money and influence to the city, and expanding suffrage and abolishing slavery put that money and influence into the hands of a larger portion of its non-aristocratic inhabitants. New York was becoming increasingly democratic, offering its diverse and teeming populace a potential for upward mobility.

These and other changes made New York a natural place not only for aspiring entrepreneurs to gravitate, but budding intellectuals as well. It was already the center of American print culture, and writers like the poet William Cullen Bryant and novelist James Fenimore Cooper were carving out places for themselves in literary history as residents of New York. Many of

America's chief painters were also moving to the city, where they earned a living painting portraits of New York's merchant elite and government higher-ups. John Trumbull, the first big-name artist to have a studio in Manhattan, served as president of the newly formed American Academy, which was headquartered in the city and promoted the growth of the fine arts. And New York was already on its way to becoming a mecca for the performing arts: Steven Price managed the Park Theater, which pioneered in bringing European talent to the American stage, a practice which spurred the growth of many actors, dancers, and singers by giving them a first-hand experience of the rich theatrical traditions of the continent.

The boom in the city's cultural life can be discerned in the attention Europe's literati were beginning to accord it. Alexis de Tocqueville arrived in New York harbor on May 11, 1831, with the intention of studying Sing Sing, the large new prison the state had opened after the closing of Newgate, an older prison that had been located in Manhattan. Initially he was enthralled by New York, praising its attractive shoreline and nicely built houses. de Tocqueville grew less enchanted with American culture during his visit, but not less interested in its growth, and he eventually published two volumes of reflections on life in the United States under the title *Democracy in America*. It was New York's architecture that prompted Tocqueville to critique American materialism: he notes with approval the evidence of the "classic" influence on some of the city's buildings, but then relates how upon closer inspection it turns out that the walls are made not of marble but of "whitewashed brick, and its columns of painted wood." Surprised by such superficiality, de Tocqueville remarks upon the tendency in America's democratic society to withdraw the arts "from the delineation of the soul to fix them exclusively on that of the body, and ... substitute the representation of motion and sensation for that of sentiment and thought; in a word, they put the real in the place of the ideal" (de Tocqueville 52).

A decade later New York received a visit from another

reputable foreign author. Charles Dickens made his first of two trips to New York, and he recorded his experience of the city in *American Notes*, a travelogue he published in 1842. Dickens's arrival was greeted with enthusiasm, especially by the swelling ranks of the city's literati, and on February 14, 1842, the "Boz Ball," an extravaganza attended by over 3,000 guests, was held to welcome him. Dickens's *Notes* record an admiration for the growing metropolis, but he was never one to ignore the plight of the less fortunate, and he documented the squalors of life in the streets and prisons with his characteristic plangency:

> What place is this, to which the squalid street conducts us? A kind of square of leprous houses, some of which are attainable only by crazy wooden stairs without. What lies beyond this tottering flight of steps, that creak beneath our tread?—a miserable room, lighted by one dim candle, and destitute of all comfort, save that which may be hidden in a wretched bed. Beside it, sits a man: his elbows on his knees: his forehead hidden in his hands. "What ails that man?" asks the foremost officer. "Fever," he sullenly replies, without looking up. Conceive the fancies of a feverish brain, in such a place as this! (Dickens 137)

This scene is drawn from Dickens's "plunge into the Five Points," an area so notoriously filthy and dangerous at the time that he regards a police escort as necessary to entering it even during the daytime. The effects of this and other such scenes in the *Notes* are intensified by juxtaposition with glowing accounts of life for the richly arrayed upper-class women and dapper businessmen who pass their days on Wall Street and Broadway, that "great promenade and thoroughfare," and among the numerous theaters and fashionable hotels (128).

The contrastive patternings Dickens calls on to describe New York inform the political, social, and economic histories of the city in the decades leading up to the Civil War as well. Here were rich dandies and poor laborers, old-boy networks and Irish gangs, Protestants and Catholics, rakish high livers and church-wardenly temperance advocates, Whigs and Barnburners, all cheek-by-jowl with one another in America's fastest-growing metropolis. By and large the tendency toward polarization was set in motion by the city's phenomenal wealth, the apportioning of which was hotly contested and rarely balanced. Railroads—the Harlem, the New York, and the Erie—were constructed in the 1830s, increasing New York's connections to the raw materials raised, hunted, mined, chopped, and caught in its hinterlands. The telegraph was invented in 1837 by native New Yorker Samuel Morse, and by the 1840s cable lines had been laid between Governor's Island and Manhattan, and Manhattan and Philadelphia. Steam packet service was established between New York and Europe in 1839, making transatlantic business flow more easily and quickly. The stages that had once taxied the city's consumers from shop to shop had been replaced by omnibuses by the 1830s, and by streetcars by the 1850s. Among the most important municipal improvements to be initiated in antebellum New York, and one of the most visible indicators of the city's prosperity, was the creation of Central Park, a 760- acre green space approved by the state legislature in 1853. Frederick Law Olmstead and Calvert Vaux won the national contest for the design of the park in 1857, and work coordinated by the aptly named Andrew Green, president of the Park Commission, commenced soon thereafter.

However, the city's apparent prosperity caused an astonishingly rapid and disorganized population expansion to occur, due both to high birth rates and a massive influx of immigrants. Charitable organizations were formed in response. There was John McDowell's New York Magdalen Society, founded in 1836 to help the city's prostitutes; Thomas Eddy and John Griscom's New York House of Refuge, founded in 1842 to help the city's youth; the Association for Improving the Condition of the Poor, founded in 1848, and other such institutions, but there were also over one million Irish immigrants in the decade between 1845 and 1855, as well hundreds of thousands of Germans, English, Scots, and Jews that immigrated to the United States the same decade, nearly three quarters of whom came by way of New York City. By 1860, more than half of the city's populace had been born abroad. The need to house this huge influx of new residents—comprised mainly of poor refugees from famines and oppressive regimes in Europe—provided the impetus for the building of tenements in Lower Manhattan, and, in turn, caused crime and disease to skyrocket. Cholera, typhoid fever, and typhus swept through the slums in the 1830s, 40s and 50s, where unspeakably poor sanitation and cramped living situations were virtually inescapable. In the Five Points area Dickens visited, the city's very first tenement, a brewery converted into apartments in 1837, was the setting for an average of one murder per night over a three-year period (Lankevich 72). Gangs called the Dead Rabbits, the Bowery Boys, and the True Blue Americans dominated the streets, making the area difficult to police. The average population density in the neighborhoods below Canal Street was 272 people per block by 1850.

The waves of European immigrants to New York in the mid-19th century imparted to the city a pair of contrasting yet equally applicable images, images that were to govern the literary discourses devoted to the city forever after. The crowded tenements, on the one hand, helped to give rise to a notion of the city as a dark labyrinth in which only the strong survive and a sense of radical alienation and disillusionment prevail. On the other hand, the strength of the hope for a better life that immigrants brought with them, as well as the sheer cultural diversity of the place, helped give rise to an alternative, utopian notion of New York as a place of extraordinary promise and opportunity, a place in which people could experience a sense of connection with one another on a scale not possible elsewhere. New York's literary history following the first vast waves of immigrants is in large part a record of the way these two images of the city commingle with and critique one another. Nowhere do these opposed images of the city receive fuller, subtler, or more influential expression than in the works of Herman Melville and Walt Whitman—perhaps the two greatest writers the city ever produced.

HERMAN MELVILLE

Melville was born August 19, 1819, in a house on Pearl Street, the second son of Allan and Maria Gansevoort Melville. Allan came from a good Boston family whose roots went back to Scottish nobility. Allan's father Thomas was a Princeton graduate who'd taken part in the Boston Tea Party and fought at Bunker Hill. Maria came from a family of wealthy Dutch patroons from Albany. Like Allan's father, Maria's was a hero of the Revolution—Peter Gansevoort, who had defended Fort Stanwix against the British. After Herman was born the family changed addresses frequently—from Pearl to Courtland, from Courtland to Bleeker, from Bleeker to Broadway—in accordance with the successes and failures of Allan's dry goods business. Allan went bankrupt in 1830, forcing the family to retreat to the Gansevoort stronghold in Albany. Herman was just 13 when his father died in 1832, at the age of 50, of pneumonia. Herman eventually took an engineering degree at Lansingburgh Academy. His failure to get a position drove him to sign on as a cabin boy on the *St. Lawrence*, a merchant ship from New York bound for Liverpool, in 1839. In 1841 he shipped on the whaler *Acushnet* for the South Seas; there he jumped ship and joined the U.S. Navy before returning to the States to start a career as an author in 1843. He lived in New York on Fourth Avenue between 1847 and 1850, and then again, having found work in the Customs House, from 1863 until his death in 1891 at 104 East 26th Street.

The two works of fiction by Melville in which New York figures most significantly are a novel, *Pierre*, published in 1852, and a masterpiece of a short story entitled "Bartleby, the Scrivener," published in *Putnam's* magazine in 1853. Both works carry in them the disillusionment Melville experienced in the wake of the commercial failure of *Moby-Dick*, his magnum opus, which had been published in 1851. That both works are set in New York not only suggests that Melville had his father's business failure on his mind, but also that the city was beginning to come into the reputation it holds today, as America's most important arena of literary and commercial activity. *Moby-Dick* itself begins in New York, where it figures as a city full of people entranced by dreams of lofty accomplishment and high endeavor—grandeurs of ambition symbolized by the ocean: "Posted like silent sentinels all around town, stand thousands upon thousands of mortal men fixed in ocean reveries. Some leaning against the piles; some seated upon the pier-heads; some looking over the bulwarks of ships from China; some high aloft in the rigging, as if striving to get a still better seaward peep." New York is the city in which, says Ishmael, "Right and left, the streets take you waterward," toward both severe risk and limitless opportunity (*Moby-Dick* 3–4).

In *Pierre* and "Bartleby" New York figures as a scene of frustrated hopes and self-alienation—themes that must have come naturally to Melville in his disappointment over the poor sales and lukewarm critical reception of *Moby-Dick*. The full title of *Pierre* is *Pierre; or, The Ambiguities*, and the subtitle underscores the connection between the uncertainty and mystification that Pierre Glendinning, the novel's protagonist, experiences and the labyrinthine urban environment that serves as a setting for his story. Pierre is a provincial innocent and aspiring writer from Saddle Meadows who pretends to wed his half-sister Isabel, born out of wedlock, in order to conceal her parentage and thus protect the family name from dishonor. Lucy Tartan, to whom Pierre had been engaged, and Delly, a servant, accompany Pierre and Isabel to New York, where Pierre intends to earn a living as a writer and support them all. But the move from the upstate New York countryside to New York City proves ruinous. Melville is out to critique the individualism, vulgarity, and chaos of the emphatically democratic society of the city by contrasting it with the aristocratic values—family history, privilege, learning, order—of the country: "... the town is the more plebeian portion: which, besides many other things, is plainly evinced by the dirty unwashed face perpetually worn by the town; but the country, like the Queen, is ever attended by scrupulous lady's maids in the guise of the seasons, and the town hath but one dress of brick turned up with stone" (*Pierre* 13). Melville somewhat heavy handedly drives his point home about the horrors of the urban by incorporating into the novel a slew of tragic deaths: Pierre kills Lucy's brother, Pierre's mother and Lucy both die, and Pierre and Isabel end up committing suicide in his prison cell in the Tombs. *Pierre; or, The Ambiguities* presents an account of New York as a sprawling infernal underworld whose promises of recognition and fortune prove, as they had for Melville in the case of *Moby-Dick*, disastrously false.

"Bartleby, the Scrivener" partakes of the same complex of concerns that *Pierre* does. Its central character is someone who goes to New York, writes, fails, is arrested, and ends up dying in the Tombs of a suicidal disinclination to eat, but the character handles these concerns with more subtlety and originality than the earlier, longer work does. "Bartleby" is less the outlashing at the New York publishing scene that *Pierre* was, and more of a diagnosis, delivered in the form of a parable, of the extent of Melville's own resolve *not to* write the kind of conventional adventure novel the public seemed to expect of him, much like Bartleby refuses to do the routine copying the narrator hires him for. The narrator is a kindhearted, mild-mannered lawyer who is proud of having done business with John Jacob Astor—one of the city's most wealthy residents, who'd made a fortune in New York real estate. He hires Bartleby to work for him as a copyist and sets him up, significantly, in a desk that faces "a window which originally had afforded a lateral view of certain grimy back-yards and bricks, but which, owing to subsequent erections, commanded at present no view at all" ("Bartleby" 110). After doing some work, "silently, palely, mechanically," for the narrator, Bartleby begins to respond to subsequent orders with his peculiar, disarmingly simple refusal: "I would prefer not to" (111–12). The narrator is bewildered as to how to handle Bartleby, who, it turns out, is living in the office at night. The last thing he wants to do is hurt Bartleby, or have him arrested, since his refusal isn't defiant or personal, and dismissing him seems ridiculous anyway: "I should have as soon thought of turning my pale, plaster-of-paris bust of Cicero out of doors" (112). The narrator decides to relocate his office; the new tenants find Bartleby on the premises, and reluctantly have him arrested and sent to the Tombs. There the narrator visits him and tries to raise his spirits, but Bartleby remains implacable; he refuses to eat and dies. The only clue the narrator is able to turn up is as provocative as it is inconclusive:

> ... Bartleby had been a subordinate clerk in the Dead Letter Office at Washington, from which he had been suddenly removed by a change in administration ... Dead letters! Does it not sound like dead men? Conceive a man by nature and misfortune prone to pallid hopelessness, can any business seem more fitted to heighten it than that of continually handling these dead letters, and assorting them for the flames?... On errands of life, these letters sped to death.... Ah, Bartleby! Ah, humanity! (140)

Incorporated into Melville's short "Story of Wall-street" are a host of concerns that in the 1850s were beginning to bedevil New York—the kind of building sprees that left viewless office windows of clerks like Bartleby, the complexity of tenant-landlord relationships, the difficulties of nonconformity in a city driven by commercial enterprise. The story's impenetrability, and its genius, inhere in the way it blends social concerns like these with the personal issues Melville faced as an artist, such as the nature of the relationship between a self-alienated, stubborn, eccentric genius ("Ah, Bartleby!") and his readership ("Ah, humanity!").

WALT WHITMAN

It was an issue Walt Whitman must have felt as well, as his tropes of identification and embrasure suggest. The way to relate to the increasing swarms of New Yorkers—and by extension, Americans, as ethnically and culturally and socially diverse as they were—was to express an intimacy with all of them, but without eliding the ideological and circumstantial differences that made them unique individuals. Hence the notoriously lengthy, beautiful catalogues: "The blab of the pave, tires of carts, sluff of boot-soles, talk of the promenaders,/The heavy omnibus, the driver with his interrogating thumb, the clank of the shod horses on the granite floor,/The now-sleighs, clinking, shouted jokes,

Whitman on Whitman

Walt Whitman knew that if his book was going to reach the public he loved and embraced in his poems, it would be necessary to take some care of its reception. Serving as his own critical "Kosmos," Whitman anonymously celebrated himself and sang himself with his characteristic gusto in reviews in three different papers: the *United States Review*, the Brooklyn *Daily Times*, and the *American Phrenological Journal*.

Some of the self-confidence evident in the reviews must have been inspired by Ralph Waldo Emerson's high praise of *Leaves* in a July 1855 letter to Whitman. "I find it the most extraordinary piece of wit and wisdom that America has yet contributed. I am very happy in reading it, as great power makes us happy," wrote Whitman's hero: "I greet you at the beginning of a great career" (Kaplan 202–3). Understandably proud, Whitman saw to it that the letter got printed in the New York *Tribune*, though he conveniently neglected to secure Emerson's consent. Interestingly, Whitman's own reviews affirmed what many of his critics asserted against him. The "author" was "one of the roughs, pelts of snow-balls,/The hurrahs for popular favorites, the fury of rous'd mobs..." (Whitman 195). Where Melville saw New York under the aspect of nightmare, as a kind of infernal maze of symbolic walls, rife with corrupting influences and inscrutable characters, Whitman, the loafing "poet of reality," saw it under the aspect of daydream, albeit an exalted kind of daydream; Whitman's New York is less obviously clouded by anxiety, less weighted with allegory, a panoramic flux of people and things whose most important common traits are an innate beauty and a susceptibility to the radical sympathy of the poet.

Whitman was born in West Hills, a rural Long Island hamlet, on May 31, 1819, to Walter Sr. and Louisa Van Velsor

large, proud, affectionate, eating, drinking, and breeding, his costume manly and free, his face sunburnt and bearded...," he wrote of himself in the *United States Review* (Gay Wilson Allen 14). "Politeness this man has none, and regulation he has none," he wrote in the Brooklyn *Times* (15). Of course, in Whitman's book, these qualities are virtues, not vices: if *Leaves of Grass* gave evidence of "New York rowdyism," as one reviewer complained, Whitman was happy to turn the idea around and accept the critique as a compliment (6). One of the roughs himself, he knew what the roughs really wanted, opinions of all predictably ruffled reviewers notwithstanding. "Where are the gristle and beards, and broad breasts, and space and ruggedness, and nonchalance, that the souls of the people love?" he ambitiously asked of the whole American literary tradition in the *United States Review* (15). Fortunately for any readers who might not have seen Emerson's letter reprinted in the *Tribune*, there was someone else who knew the answer quite well.

Whitman. His father was a taciturn carpenter of English descent, his mother a loving homemaker who came from a family of Dutch Quakers. In May of 1823 the family moved to Brooklyn, which at the time occupied a happy medium between the burgeoning metropolis of Manhattan to the west and the quiet villages of Long Island to the east: it was a city of 7,000 when the Whitmans arrived, though it grew rapidly due to its proximity to Manhattan and became the nation's fourth largest city by the time the Civil War broke out. His early education was compounded of an admixture of the grammar and arithmetic lessons he received at District School No. 1, on Concord and Adams Streets, and the Quakerism and progressive political thought—his father had known Thomas Paine and subscribed to the *Free Enquirer*, a radical journal—he absorbed at home through his parents. At the age of 11 he left school to help support his family, and so began his haphazard juggernaut through a notably varied series of jobs: office boy for a pair of Brooklyn lawyers; apprentice editor at the *Long Island Patriot*; compositor for the *Long-Island Star*; journeyman school-teacher; founder and editor of the *Long-Islander*; typesetter for the *Long Island Democrat*; journeyman printer in Manhattan; author (of a temperance novel entitled *Franklin Evans*); editor of *The Brooklyn Daily Eagle* (a major newspaper with Democratic affiliations); reporter for the *New Orleans Daily Crescent*; founder and editor of the *Brooklyn Freeman*; print-shop owner, editor of the *New York Daily News*; guidebook writer (*The Salesman's and Traveler's Directory for Long Island*); reporter for William Cullen Bryant's *Evening Post*; president of the Brooklyn Art Union; carpenter; and then, in the summer of 1855, author of a slim book of untitled poems he called *Leaves of Grass*.

Though it was not until years later that Whitman wrote the book's connections to New York into "Song of Myself" by proclaiming Manhattan his origin—"Walt Whitman, a kosmos, of Manhattan the son," *Leaves of Grass*, in spite of its pastoral title, teems with the life of the city (210). He acknowledges this relationship directly in *Specimen Days* as he reflects on riding buses on Broadway: "...the influence of those Broadway omnibus jaunts and drivers and declamations and escapades undoubtedly enter'd into the gestation of 'Leaves of Grass'" (703). The importance of New York to *Leaves of Grass* is inestimable because Whitman felt the city's influence on so many levels, both conceptually and stylistically. Its material culture connects to his celebration of the physical; its abundance of sights and sounds connects to his long lines and catalogues; the city's ethnic and social diversity connects to his egalitarianism; and so on. And it is Whitman's absorption of so much of New York— its materialism, its sensory abundance, its diverse population, among so much else, that prompts him to perhaps his most influential invention, his recognition of a self that stands apart from the city's bustling energies:

> Trippers and askers surround me,
> People I meet .... the effect upon me of my early life ....
>   of the ward and city I live in .... of the nation,
> The latest news .... discoveries, inventions, societies ....
>   authors old and new,
> My dinner, dress, associates, looks, business, compliments,
>   dues,
> The real or fancied indifference of some man or woman I love,
> The sickness of one of my folks—or of myself .... or ill-doing
>   .... or loss or lack of money .... or depressions or
>   exhaltations,
> They come to me days and nights and go from me again,
> But they are not the Me myself.
>
> Apart from the pulling and hauling stands what I am,
> Stands amused, complacent, compassionating, idle, unitary,
> Looks down, is erect, bends an arm on an impalpable certain
>   rest,
> Looks with sidecurved head curious what will come next,
> Both in and out of the game, and watching and wondering
>   at it. (191)

The life of New York—its "trippers and askers," its "news," its "business"—compels Whitman to discover an aboriginal self-hood he calls "the Me myself." The "Me myself" is fully estranged from the city's routines, standing "apart from the pulling and hauling," yet not at a distance so remote that it carries the idea of rejection: he "stands amused, complacent, compassionating, idle, unitary," he is "curious what will come next."

Whitman added "Crossing Brooklyn Ferry," which was orig-inally entitled "Sun-Down Poem," to *Leaves of Grass* in 1856. It is fitting that New York's greatest poem should take its own audience as its central concern, for in the city's massive, informed readership lies perhaps its chief claim to being the cultural capital of America. Crossing westward—a direction that resonates with the westward expansion of the country that was so much at issue in the 1850s—over the East River, Whitman audaciously identifies himself not only with his cur-rent audience but with the audiences he will know in the future as well: "It avails not, time nor place—distance avails not,/I am with you, you men and women of a generation, or ever so many generations hence,/Just as you feel when you look on the river and sky, so I felt,/Just as any of you is one of a living crowd, I was one of a crowd..." (308–9). He makes this identi-fication persuasive by presenting his impressions of New York on the Emersonian assumption that what he notices and thinks is what everyone notices and thinks, but rarely if ever voices. Though Whitman has been criticized for seeming to ignore New York's dark side, in section 6 of "Crossing Brooklyn Ferry" he strengthens his identification with his readers by building into it a moving gesture of consolation: "It is not upon you alone the dark patches fall,/The dark threw its patches down upon me also... Nor is it you alone who know what it is to be evil,/I am he who knew what it was to be evil,/I too knitted the old knot of contrariety,/Blabb'd, blush'd, resented, lied, stole, grudg'd,/Had guile, anger, lust, hot wishes I dared not speak...". (311). The radical humanity evinced in lines like these makes Whitman's ghostly gesture of intimacy with his future readers powerfully compelling: "Who knows, for all the distance, but I am as good as looking at you now, for all you cannot see me?" (312).

CHAPTER FOUR

Toward Greater
New York

"What is it then between us?" Whitman asked in "Crossing Brooklyn Ferry," alluding to the "distance" between himself and his readers, and also, during a time of such intense concern about the fate of an increasingly divided America, to distances of several other kinds as well—between the North and the South, between the concerns of the nation's merchant classes and the needs of its poor immigrants, between Republicans and Democrats. "Whatever it is, it avails not," Whitman had courageously announced, hoping to produce in his readers a recognition of their own common humanity. But Whitman, though he presided over a rowdy table of bohemian writers and artists at Pfaff's Tavern, located just north of Bleeker Street on Broadway, was still relatively unknown, and the power of his eloquence would not sway his nation from its course toward Civil War.

Whitman's New York rattled and hummed with the sounds of political discord. With each new candidate, law, and act came a blur of slogans and a complex realignment of allegiances. Though New York was home to people who occupied every point on the moral compass surrounding the issues of slavery and secession, the city's needle predictably found its true north in the almighty dollar: its powerful merchants carried on a brisk business with the southern states, and they didn't want to see that lucrative alliance damaged by war. Tammany Hall Democrats were already beginning to dominate city politics, and although Abraham Lincoln thrilled a massive audience organized by influential newsmen Horace Greeley and William Cullen Bryant at Cooper Union during his campaign in 1860, Lincoln was a Republican who adamantly opposed slavery, and the majority of the city voted against him in the election. After Lincoln was elected—he had won New York as a result of Republican support upstate—the city was forced to confront the implications of war for its trade with the south. With its harbor full of clipper ships, New York dominated the nation's foreign commerce, and two-thirds of American imports and one third of its exports came through the city. It was the port's control over trade with proportions like these, and the threat to that trade that Lincoln's election posed, that motivated Mayor Fernando Wood to urge the Common Council to consider declaring independence for the city. Freed from federal tariffs and the meddlesome state legislature, New York City, Wood argued, could pursue and strengthen profitable trade relations with all the states, northern, southern, and those yet to come out west. But when word reached the city that the Confederacy's plans allowed for its cities to import European goods without the heavy duties the federal government forced New York to levy, opening the way for cheaper trade via southern ports, Wood dropped the idea of municipal secession and decided to support the war.

CIVIL WAR YEARS

A week after the Confederates fired on Fort Sumter in Charleston harbor on April 12, 1861, and fence-sitting northerners like Wood were forced to recognize that war had finally come, hundreds of thousands of New Yorkers assembled in Union Square to ratify the formation of the Union Defense Committee, an association of city merchants who would oversee the financing of the war effort. Days later, regiments were already forming and being dispatched to Washington, D.C. Especially enthusiastic to enlist were the city's immigrants. Germans, Hungarians, Swiss, Polish, and Italian companies formed, eager to escape the hard economic times that the trade rupture with the South had caused and to silence nativist polemicists with a bold show of patriotism. Thousands of Irish-Americans, who had the bonus incentive of delivering an indirect blow against England by fighting their Confederate allies, also joined up. Meanwhile the Union Defense Committee funneled millions of the city's dollars into military supplies and transportation, and into relief funds for the families of volunteers. New York sent nearly 100 regiments into battle in 1861 alone, honoring soldiers' departure with great fanfare.

War sent New York's economy into an awkward climb. Values fluctuated as news of victories and defeats came back from the battlefields, but the net result for the stock exchange was growth. Wheat, lumber, cattle, and oil came into the city from the Great Lakes region by way of an expanding network of railroads. Iron works and shipbuilding yards boomed as contracts for outfitting and repairing the Union fleet came in. In Brooklyn, production of drugs and medical supplies escalated in plants run by Charles Pfizer and Edward Robinson Squibb in order to meet demands created by the war. Brooks Brothers clothiers made its first big sale to the New York State Military Board early in the war by filling an order for more than 10,000 new uniforms. Newspapers like *Harper's Weekly* and *New York Illustrated News* carried sketches and etchings by Currier and Ives depicting battlefields with a graphic immediacy that sent sales soaring by tapping into the city's illiterate population. New York bankers knit themselves more tightly into the fabric of the federal government by helping it to manage its war debts.

In spite of the horrific news coming back from the front lines, or perhaps spurred by it, New Yorkers took advantage of wartime prosperity to indulge a craving for luxury. Millionaires proliferated in the city, and they paraded their wealth by riding around Central Park in velvet coats and camel hair shawls on Sundays. The rich dined out at Lorenzo Delmonico's at Fifth and 14th, hosted fancy balls, or drank all night at the Rotunda Bar in Astor House. First Lady Mary Lincoln regularly joined the throngs pouring through New York's department stores: in one instance, she overspent a 20,000 dollar budget to redecorate the White House and then begged government officials to keep her extravagance secret from her husband. A.T. Stewart's "New Store" stood as the central emblem of the city's new appetite for fashion. A white cast-iron building five stories tall and glinting with 2,000 panes of plate glass in its windows, the store employed nearly 1,000 cashiers, clerks, porters, seamstresses, and dressmakers to bring their customers the finest in silks, linens, and ball get-ups.

But the tale told by the numbers in the books of retailers, bankers, and industry executives, and illustrated in the partying and promenading of Fifth Avenue millionaires, was not the tale of the city's lower classes. Enthusiasm for the war waned in 1862 and 1863 for a number of reasons, chief among them the gruesome reality of the unprecedented loss of life occurring on the battlefields. Union army leaders were frequently corrupt or incompetent men who'd risen to positions of leadership through connections rather than on the basis of professional training or experience. Trouble financing the war led the government to print paper money, which in turn led to inflation, which out-stripped wage increases for the city's working classes. Building projects declined, leaving the housing situation worse than ever. Laborers began to unite, but employers broke up strikes by drawing on New York's hard-up African-American population as scabs, infusing the turmoil with an explosive racial element.

On January 1, 1863, President Lincoln issued the Emancipation Proclamation, stirring up still more resentment against the war. Antiwar activists argued that freeing slaves would ruin the economy by reducing America's ability to compete with Brazil and Cuba, which still relied on slave labor. The Proclamation hit especially close to home for laborers, who feared losing their jobs to freed slaves. Democrats urging reconciliation with the South waged an intense pamphlet war against Republicans of the Union League Club—comprised of New York's wealthy businessmen and politicians—during the spring and early summer of 1863, stirring up social and racial tensions with a flurry of rhetoric. It was under these heated circumstances that the National Conscription Act—including a notorious clause that allowed rich draftees to buy their way out of military duty for a fee of $300—went into effect on Saturday, July 11, 1863.

New York's working class population protested the draft the following Monday, July 13, initiating a riot that would take four bloody days to run its course. Early in the morning crowds of laborers streamed into the streets and marched on the marshal's office on Third Avenue. The "No Draft" signs they held expressed the kind of non-violent resistance they must have had in mind, but a company of firemen arrived and upped the ante. Angry at being deprived of their customary exemption from military duty, they stoned the office windows, drenched the building in turpentine and set it on fire, then drove off other companies that arrived to fight the blaze. The mob's main targets were the rich, who could afford to buy their way out of service; the Republicans, who supported the draft; and African-Americans, whose newly declared freedom would drive down wages and increase competition for jobs.

All over the city mobs formed, armed, and went on the offensive. Trains were stoned and railroad tracks wrenched out of line; telegraph poles were cut down and homes torched. The headquarters of Republican newspapers like the *Tribune* and the *Times* were attacked, as were the offices of noted Republicans like Charles King, President of Columbia College, and Mayor George Opdyke. Violence against the city's black population was especially vicious. Boardinghouses, bars, and tenements that catered to blacks were hailed with paving stones and burnt; crowds lynched and burned several black men; the Colored

Orphan Asylum on Fifth and 43rd was ransacked and fired, though its 237 young children were able to escape. By the second day, rioters had armed themselves with homemade bombs and guns. They focused on New York's wealthy elite and their businesses. Wall Street proved too well defended for the mobs, but high-society strollers were assaulted in the streets as people yelled "There goes a $300 man," and Brooks Brothers was looted, as were other stores and banks on the southern end of the island (Burrows and Wallace 893). Crowds built barricades in the streets and skirmished with police. By Wednesday, the protest had mushroomed into a full-fledged battle, with police and volunteer militias clearing streets with howitzers and mobs strategically destroying ferries and severing telegraph lines in order to obstruct help from reinforcements. Battle-weary regiments fresh from the carnage at Gettysburg were summoned and finally arrived on Wednesday evening. They reclaimed the streets one by one, clearing each tenement house of snipers and bombers. Six thousand federal troops were in the city by Thursday night, when the riot finally ended.

The draft riot was strikingly captured in the diaries of George Templeton Strong, a well-connected New York lawyer who, like many members of the upper class, felt threatened by the massive immigrant population—especially the Irish—and the increasingly democratic political order that came with it. A member of the Union League Club and vice president of the New York Historical Society, Strong cherished the notion of an older New York with an Anglo-Dutch patrician caste managing its interests and monitoring its values. His diaries, regarded as among the greatest of any 19th-century American, follow the city's history from 1826, when Strong was sixteen, through his death in 1875. Strong's conservative leanings make him especially sensitive to New York's metamorphoses both physical and metaphysical, the quickness of which is a staple theme in the literature of the city. His entries concerning the draft riot emphasize his lack of sympathy with the protesters, and give a precise account of the confusion and distress that must have held sway among the city dignitaries who felt the violence as a direct blow to the economic, political, and social order they represented:

> The rabble was perfectly homogeneous. Every brute in the drove was pure Celtic—hod-carrier or loafer. They were unarmed. A few carried pieces of fence-paling and the like. They turned off west into Forty-fifth Street and gradually collected in front of two three-story dwelling houses on Lexington Avenue ... Nobody could tell why these houses were singled out ... The mob was in no hurry; they had no need to be; there was no one to molest them or make them afraid. The beastly ruffians were masters of the situation and of the city. After a while sporadic paving-stones began to fly at the windows, ladies and children emerged from the rear and had a rather hard scramble over a high board fence, and then scudded off across the open, Heaven knows whither. Then men and small boys appeared at rear windows and began smashing the sashes and the blinds and shied out light articles, such as books and crockery, and dropped chairs and mirrors into the back yard; the rear fence was demolished and loafers were seen marching off with portable articles of furniture. And at last a light smoke began to float out of the windows and I came away. I could endure the disgraceful, sickening sight no longer, and what could I do? (Strong 335–36)

The "perfect" homogeneity of the Irish "rabble" is given special emphasis, as it exemplifies the leveling effects of democracy Strong both deplored and found himself helpless to combat: "what could I *do*?" The rioters are represented as "brutes" and "beastly ruffians," and also, twice, as "loafers," barbaric ingrates, in Strong's view, who are too ignorant and uncivilized to understand that by sacking a mansion they're doing harm to the very economy that ostensibly sustains them. Strong points up the dangers of rule by the majority in this passage by accentuating the aimlessness of the mob's will along with the ease with which it assumes power: "Nobody could tell why these houses were singled out," but a few "sporadic paving-stones" later and people are forced to evacuate, which in turn sets the stage for looting, and, "at last," the inevitable fire. At the end of the riot, on July 16th, in his diary Strong voices the hope that New Yorkers will have learned something from the experience, but goes on to speculate that New York's massive crowds are just too large to be susceptible to instruction by their own history, too varied to be anything other than changeful. That the forgetful "people" he has in mind here are mainly foreign-born Americans is implied by the trope of the shoreline he employs: immigrants, like grains of sand, are numberless, and continually wash ashore by the same natural process that sweeps their collective memory smooth: "Every impression that's made on our people passes away so soon, almost as if stamped on the sand of a sea-beach. Were our moods a little less fleeting, I should have great hope of permanent good from the general wrath these outrages provoked ... But we shall forget all about it before next November" (340).

Life returned to normal fairly quickly in the city, due largely to actions taken by Democrats and Boss Tweed of Tammany Hall to temper the severity of the conscription law. They got Lincoln to decrease the quota he was calling for, and they created an Exemption Committee, which dispensed millions to poor draftees with families to support and municipal workers so that they could buy substitutes and pay fees. Relief efforts aided blacks as well. The Merchants' Committee for the Relief of Colored People Suffering from the Late Riots was created to dole out clothing and money to the several thousand workers who had not fled the island in the wake of the violence. The Union League saw to it that a regiment of black soldiers was formed: on March 5, 1864, the Twentieth Regiment United States Colored Troops marched at a rally in Union Square on their way to New Orleans.

New York's economy returned to its full strength quickly too, as the war boom continued through 1864 and 1865. Congress legalized trade in cotton with the Confederacy and New York merchants quickly took advantage of it, turning huge profits. Others invested in lands out west, available at $1.25 per acre thanks to the Homestead Act. The exchange of stocks grew ever more complicated, affording brokers a wider variety of ways to profit. The establishment of the Long Room on Broad Street allowed continuous trading, enabling hundreds of transactions to occur at the same time. An Evening Exchange was opened so that trading could occur twenty-four hours a day. Investing in gold, the value of which rose or fell depending on the outcomes of battles down south, was quite popular and took place in its own chamber, the Gold Room. Using an elaborate spy network and telegraph system, brokers were able to get word of battle results and troop movements—information they turned into fortunes—before the President himself.

Three days after General Ulysses S. Grant forced General Robert E. Lee to surrender at Appomattox in Virginia—a day of massive celebration in the New York's streets—President Lincoln was shot and killed, bringing an abrupt end to the festive mood. His funeral train wended northward through Baltimore and Philadelphia and crossed the Hudson into Manhattan. After a day of mourning during which businesses and government offices closed, his body was carried in a funeral car on Broadway from City Hall to 14th Street and then over to Fifth Avenue to the Hudson River train station. The train left for Albany on the afternoon of April 25th, as the city bid Lincoln a respectful farewell.

POSTWAR NEW YORK

Political life in postwar New York was dominated by "Boss" William Tweed, grand sachem of Tammany Hall. Born into a Scottish family on April 3, 1823, Tweed left school to take part in his father's chair-manufacturing business, but later found his niche as a fireman working for the American Engine Company. Municipal services were linked closely to the Tammany organization, and Tweed was able to find his way from the fire brigade to a seat on the city's Board of Education in the 1850s. Forging alliances with influential politicians and judges right and left, Tweed then became supervisor of public works for the city and in 1860 was made chairman of the Democratic Central Committee, a position he used to gain control of Tammany Hall. In 1863 he was appointed permanent chair of Tammany's Executive Committee. The Tweed Ring made huge sums of money by demanding various kickbacks, payoffs, and fees in exchange for political offices and municipal positions and contracts. For example, the Ring made a habit of hiring Andrew J. Garvey to do plastering work in the city. With the contracts well-padded, Garvey billed the city for nearly $3,000,000 in just two years, more than half of which was kicked back to Tweed and his Tammany colleagues. In another notorious episode, Tweed padded the bill for the construction of the New York City courthouse—originally targeted as a $350,000 project—until costs totaled over $10 million, including several seven thousand-dollar thermometers, a handful of forty thousand-dollar brooms, and a half-dozen men listed on the payroll as custodial staff who were no longer alive. Tweed's particular genius was to disperse the money the Ring took in judiciously and widely, so as to implicate as many people as possible in the corruption. He was also good at cultivating a public image as a generous "man of the people," and regularly signed checks to charitable organizations and relief funds. Tammany had always catered to the masses; Tweed enhanced his image and reinforced Tammany's civic reputation by funneling money into municipal improvements of all shapes and sizes: parks were created, streets cleaned, and school budgets enlarged.

By 1871 Tweed was at the high-water mark of his career. Living in a mansion on West Thirty-sixth Street, he enjoyed his wealth by making extraordinary shows of hospitality, entertaining hoards of guests with fine food and wine. That he spent nearly a million dollars on his daughter's wedding says something of the lifestyle he enjoyed. The only sign of danger was that caricaturist Thomas Nast regularly published cartoons illustrating the shady operations the Tweed Ring engaged in. Tweed feared Nast and attempted to bribe him into stopping the cartoon series with half a million dollars, since the cartoons made him look bad to his supporters, many of whom were illiterate. Nast refused. But Nast had only laid the groundwork for a much more serious scandal that was to break later the same year. Having refused to honor Sheriff Jimmy O'Brien's request for a $250,000 payoff, the Tweed Ring found itself at O'Brien's mercy: he threatened the Ring with the publication of the records of all of their corrupt transactions. When they refused to pay up, O'Brien gave the records to George Jones, editor of the *Times*, who refused the Ring's five million dollar bribe and began publishing them in July of 1871. After months of public gatherings and committee formations, Tweed was arrested on December 16. His ring quickly disintegrated as his Tammany colleagues sought refuge in Canada and Europe. Tweed served a little more than a year of his twelve-year jail sentence before being released after a court of appeals overturned the decision against him. However, a much larger civil suit was brought against him, and he was imprisoned again. He escaped to Spain in 1875, but the Spanish government caught him and returned him to the city. He died in prison on April 12, 1878. The city was able to recover just nine hundred thousand dollars of the Ring's illegal take, which according to some estimates ran to several hundred millions.

Tweed had brought a level of corruption to New York politics not seen since its days as a remote trading post, but the city continued to grow during his reign as immigrants from northern Europe flooded in once the Civil War was over. As the merchant classes moved up and out to distance themselves from the tenements, the city expanded, and by the 1880s extended north to Forty-second Street. The rich moved to Harlem and outlying suburbs, including Brooklyn, which created a need for improved transportation. Construction on the Brooklyn Bridge, using plans developed by John Roebling and directed by John's son Washington, began in January of 1870 and was completed in May of 1883 as city residents looked on with awe. Travel between two of America's largest cities now cost a penny, and the bridge set the stage for planning Greater New York. Other conveniences, improvements, and amenities were instituted in the decades following the war as well: telephone service became available in Manhattan in the late 1870s; Thomas Edison's incandescent lights were first used to light streets in 1882; and the Metropolitan Opera House opened in 1883.

HENRY JAMES

Flourish though it did, New York couldn't offer Henry James—author of more world-class writing than any other American before or since—what he felt Europe could, and late in 1875 he moved from New York to Paris, and took up permanent residence in a London flat the following year. He was a native New Yorker, born on April 15, 1843, at 21 Washington Place. The Jameses were a cultured bunch: Henry Sr. was a thinker and an author; the family frequently traveled to Europe; Henry David Thoreau and Ralph Waldo Emerson were friends of the family; and older brother William was to achieve renown as a philosopher and psychologist. Like many upper middle-class families of the time, the Jameses regularly moved uptown as the city expanded northward, away from the increasingly crowded immigrant wards of Lower Manhattan: in 1847 they moved to 11 Fifth Avenue; the following year they moved to 58 West Fourteenth Street. As James writes in *Washington Square*, in 19th-century Manhattan, migrating up the island in order to keep up with the best society was a trend dictated by the situation of the island itself: "...the tide of fashion began to set steadily northward, as, indeed, in New York, thanks to the narrow channel in which it flows, it is obliged to do..." (James 15). Though James left the city at the age of 32, he had absorbed enough of its aura to remember it with a deeply felt nostalgia. Referring to the Washington Square area he explored as a boy, he writes that "this portion of New York appears to many persons to be the most delectable. It has a kind of established repose which is not of frequent occurrence in other quarters of the long, shrill city; it has a riper, richer, more honorable look than any of the upper ramifications of the great longitudinal thoroughfare—the look of having had something of a social history" (16).

James's career got off to a fast start. After several European tours he spent a short time at Harvard University, from which he withdrew without taking a degree, and then turned to writing stories and reviews for periodicals like *The Atlantic Monthly* and *The Nation*. With the appearance of a short novel, *Daisy Miller*, in 1878, James became an internationally known literary figure. James's fiction draws on New York frequently as a setting and as a symbol throughout his prolific career, but it is in *Washington Square*, which appeared in 1880, that the city receives its lengthiest treatment. He derived the plot from a story he heard at a party in London on February 20, 1879; Fanny Kemble, the famous actress, told James the true story of her brother's unsuccessful attempt to seduce and marry a wealthy young woman solely for her money. Her brother was a handsome wit, and the girl plain, dull, and subject to the tyrannical will of a father who disapproved of the connection. James did little to alter Kemble's tale, except to rename the characters and relocate it to the antebellum New York of his boyhood. In doing so, James gives a revealing glimpse of his mixed feelings about the city, which emerges as a place of youthful innocence but also mercenary greed, a place in which the "social history" James craved seemed worthy of his curiosity, but available only in sequestered pockets, and too susceptible to the harmful influence of a vulgar commercial spirit.

In *Washington Square* the witheringly reasonable Dr. Sloper and his peculiar, romantic sister Lavinia attempt to guide Sloper's demure, slow-witted daughter Catherine through a courtship with the debonair Morris Townshend, who means to replenish the fortune he wasted sowing his wild oats by marrying rich. Starry-eyed Aunt Lavinia can't resist encouraging the union, and goes so far as to indulge in a secret meeting with

Morris, acting as Catherine's agent, though she really has very little counsel to offer him: "When Morris at last arrived, they sat together for half an hour in the duskiest corner of the back shop; and it is hardly too much to say that this was the happiest half hour that Mrs. Penniman had known for years. The situation was really thrilling, and it scarcely seemed to her a false note when her companion asked for an oyster stew, and proceeded to consume it before her eyes" (88–89). Dr. Sloper, however, reads the overall situation like a receipt, and states his reasons for vetoing the relationship to Morris with an authoritative clarity: "Your absence of means, of a profession, of visible resources or prospects, places you in a category from which it would be imprudent for me to select a husband for my daughter, who is a weak young woman with a large fortune. In any other capacity I am perfectly prepared to like you. As a son-in-law, I abominate you" (68).

Divided between her father's realism and her aunt's romanticism, Catherine remains neutral, becoming in the end an outwardly cheerful old maid, mindful of the simpler values and customs of an older New York: "From her own point of view the great facts of her career were that Morris Townshend had trifled with her affection, and that her father had broken its spring. Nothing could ever alter these facts.... There was something dead in her life, and her duty was to try to fill the void" (187–88). Evident, perhaps, in Catherine's dispassionate perception of her "career" is James's own perception of New York, and America in general, as a site of diminished dramatic possibilities, at least in contrast to Europe, whose richer culture and longer history might furnish a novelist with more complex raw materials. New York's history, in James's view—or, rather, in one of James's views—was all too predictable, its progress so closely tied to making money that it could be allegorized in the linear migration of its nouveau riche families. As Catherine's cousin Arthur puts it: "That's the way to live in New York: to move every three or four years. Then you always get the last thing. It's because the city's growing so quick—you've got to keep up with it. It's going straight uptown—that's where New York's going. If I wasn't afraid Marian would be lonely, I'd go up there—right to the top—and wait for it" (27).

With or without the endorsement of James's residence in town, New York would displace Boston—stomping ground of the Transcendentalists—permanently as the literary center of the nation in the last quarter of the 19th-century, a fact emphatically confirmed by William Dean Howell's choice to move to New York from Boston, where the author of *The Rise of Silas Lapham* had thrived for decades as a writer, in the late 1880s. Born in 1837 in Ohio, Howells went on to serve as a consul in Italy, and upon his return to the States in 1866 was lured to Boston by publisher James T. Fields, who enjoined him to work as an assistant editor for *The Atlantic Monthly*. *The Rise of Silas Lapham*, set in Boston, was published in 1885, and its author, comfortably ensconced in a Back Bay mansion, seemed poised to live out his life as a pillar of the literary society of that city. He suffered a breakdown however, and in the process of recovering decided to reorient his life from the perspective afforded by New York. He committed himself to Harper and Brothers publishing company, based in New York, and left Boston's *Atlantic* to become a columnist for New York's *Harper's Monthly*. By 1888 Howells was a New Yorker, overwhelmed and fascinated with the city's energy and variety: "We have been two months in New York, in this flat," he wrote to a his friend Thomas Perry, "...and I have been trying to catch on to the bigger life of the place. It's immensely interesting, but I don't know whether I shall manage it; I'm fifty-one, you know. There are lots of interesting young painting and writing fellows, and the place is lordly free, with foreign touches of all kinds all through its abounding Americanism: Boston seems of another planet" (*Life in Letters* 413).

Howells' move is allegorized in his novel *A Hazard of New Fortunes*, published in 1888. It tells the story of Basil March and his wife Isabel. Basil is an insurance agent for Reciprocity Life in Boston, and he is invited to become editor of *Every Other Week*, a new literary review, in New York. Isabel is reluctant: "...you know I don't like New York. I don't approve of it. It's so *big*, and *so* hideous!" (14). Its hideousness was probably oddly appealing to Howells, literary ancestor of naturalist novelists like Stephen Crane and Theodore Dreiser, because he was increasingly interested in a realism centered on the kind of hard facts that the Darwinian scrambling of New York's concentrated multitudes provided in such abundance. The novel culminates with a calamitous strike by streetcar workers, which Basil is sent to cover for *Every Other Week*. Conrad Dryfoos, one of Basil's colleagues at the journal, is sympathetic to the plight of the strikers, but is nonetheless killed by a stray bullet while attempting to bring peace to the situation. The tragic outcome bespeaks Howells's ambivalent desire to balance his romantic perspective with an inquiry into the harsher, more unruly version of reality that New York put in evidence with a unique intensity.

The unruly energies of the city that interested Howells (and perhaps scared James) can in many ways be traced to the waves of immigrants which continued to arrive, renewing New York's housing problems, escalating tensions stemming from ethnic differences, and alarming the well-heeled natives, but also helping to drive the city's robust economy and imparting to it a lively multicultural character. What shifted in the years between the publication of *Washington Square* and *A Hazard of New Fortunes* was the national origin of most of the immigrants: prior to 1883, about 85 percent of New York's immigrants came from northern Europe; after 1883, however, most came from Europe's southern and eastern countries—Russia, Italy, and Greece. The number of immigrants who arrived in the 1880s more than doubled that of any previous decade. It was in these years that New York began to amass its sizeable Jewish and Italian populations. Persecution initiated by Czar Alexander II sent nearly one million Russian Jews to New York by the turn of the century. The population density of the East Side Jewish quarter reached 640,000 people per square mile in 1900—at the time the highest such level recorded in world history (Lankevich 128). Southern Italians were migrating across the Atlantic at a comparable rate: whereas the city was home to only about twenty thousand Italian immigrants in 1880, there were nearly a quarter of a million by 1900.

Charitable organizations and socio-political reform could scarcely keep up with the needs of New York's many new residents. The enormous difficulties of life in Manhattan's Lower East Side, where many of the immigrants settled, was captured by Jacob Riis, a reporter for the *New York Tribune* who was himself a Danish immigrant, in *How the Other Half Lives*, which was published in 1890. By revealing the horrific conditions the city's poor were made to endure, Riis helped silence nativists who sought to pin the blame for increasing crime and disease on the immigrants themselves, rather than their crowded, filthy environment. Riis uses several strategies of representation to bring home the nature of the situation fully, among them the practice of reminding his readers how different the city once was: "Leaving the Elevated Railroad where it dives under the Brooklyn Bridge at Franklin Square, scarce a dozen steps will take us where we wish to go... We stand upon the domain of the tenement. In the shadow of the great stone abutments the old Knickerbocker houses linger like ghosts of a departed day. Down the winding slope of Cherry Street—proud and fashionable Cherry Hill that was—their broad steps, sloping roofs, and dormer windows are easily made out; all the more easily for the contrast with the ugly barracks that elbow them right and left" (Riis 22). Another of Riis's more effective gestures is to invite the reader *in*—into an alley, a saloon, a tenement: "...we grope our way up the stairs and down from floor to floor, listening to the sounds behind the closed doors—some of quarrelling, some of coarse songs, more of profanity. They are true. When the summer heats come with their suffering they have meaning more terrible than words can tell. Come over here. Step carefully over this baby—it is a baby, spite of its rags and dirt—under these iron bridges called fire-escapes, but loaded down, despite the incessant watchfulness of the firemen, with broken household goods, with wash-tubs and barrels, over which no man could climb from a fire. This gap between dingy brick-walls is a yard. That strip of smoke-colored sky up there is the heaven of these people" (34).

If You Can Read This, You're Fired

Horace Greeley's New York *Tribune* was one of the most widely read newspapers in America in the 1800s. Greeley himself was very influential—both as an editor and as a writer of editorial columns. His reputation for insisting upon accurate reporting was legendary in his own day.

Ironically, his zeal for exactitude coexisted with a penchant for writing illegibly. In one episode, Joseph Bucklin Bishop, a Tribune reporter, erroneously reported the results of a local election. Greeley, who could tell by the number of voters in Bishop's story that there must have been a mistake, reprimanded Bishop and then handed him a scribbled dismissal note. Shaken by Greeley's outburst, Bishop showed the note to another editor, who, unable to make out what it said, told him to ignore it and keep on working. Greeley never seemed to recall that he had fired Bishop.

Apparently, Bishop's experience was not unique: Greeley regularly wrote illegible dismissals, firing some employees over and over again, without ever noticing that they often continued working at the *Tribune*. In many cases—perhaps ones in which Greeley's wrath was conveyed adequately enough in person to make his handwriting irrelevant—newly fired reporters took the chicken-scratch dismissals to the offices of other newspapers and used them, successfully, as recommendations from Greeley (Hall 80–81).

STEPHEN CRANE

It was this New York that another journalist, Stephen Crane, sought to portray in his novel, *Maggie: A Girl of the Streets*, which appeared in 1893. William Dean Howells, Crane's mentor, helped Crane find a publisher for the book, which he admired, but Crane surpassed Howells in his commitment to depicting what Riis called "the other half" in a manner unmitigated by the conventions of romance and picturesque. With *Maggie* Crane inaugurated the tradition of American Naturalism, which fused a style of detailed observation borrowed from writers like Howells and the French novelist Emile Zola with the principles of Darwin's theory of evolution, and is exemplified in the writings of New York writers like Theodore Dreiser, John Dos Passos, Ralph Ellison, and Norman Mailer. The novel's heroine is Maggie Johnson of "Rum Alley," a fictional region of lower Manhattan. Brought up by an alcoholic mother and abusive father, Maggie falls prey to the charms of Pete, a bartender, who later abandons her, forcing her into prostitution, a miserable career which ends in suicide. Throughout the story, New York's tenement districts provide the dark backdrop for Maggie's struggles: "...a dozen gruesome doorways gave up loads of babies to the street and the gutter. A wind of early autumn raised yellow dust from cobbles and swirled it against a hundred windows. Long streamers of garments fluttered from fire-escapes. In all unhandy places there were buckets, brooms, rags and bottles. In the street infants played or fought with other infants or sat stupidly in the way of vehicles. Formidable women, with uncombed hair and disordered dress, gossiped while leaning on railings, or screamed in frantic quarrels. Withered persons, in curious postures of submission to something, sat smoking pipes in obscure corners" (Crane 30). The extremity of conditions in the city give Crane the impetus to critique the very notion of art itself, insofar as it makes a habit of lulling its admirers into comfortingly idealistic assumptions, as Maggie seems on the verge of recognizing during a trip to the theater: "She wondered if the culture and refinement she had seen imitated, perhaps grotesquely, by a stage heroine, could be acquired by a girl who lived in a tenement house and worked in a shirt factory" (53).

New York's huge growth during the latter half of the 19th-century sowed the seeds for its eventual expansion into Greater New York, a change finalized just before the turn of the century. Manhattan annexed the towns of Kingsbridge, West Farms, and Morrisania, which lay west of the Bronx River, in 1874, but with the construction of the Brooklyn Bridge in 1883, and the Williamsburgh Bridge in 1896, the vision many city leaders had of an augmented New York took on a new energy. Leading the charge was Andrew Green, the lawyer and preservationist who'd played an important role in creating Central Park. Green served as president of the Consolidation Inquiry Committee, a group which included the mayors of the municipalities in question and presented a report to the state government in Albany detailing the advantages that would come by merging Queens, Kings, and Richmond counties with the city. Republicans opposed the idea at first, but then were persuaded that the many conservative voters in the regions surrounding the city might help them to leverage control of the city out of the hands of the Democratic Tammany Hall, which had continued to thrive even after the disruption of the Tweed Ring. What finally decided the issue was a spreading recognition that both New York and the counties surrounding it stood to make economic gains: by joining with one another, commercial connections between the different areas would be reinforced and made more convenient, and would allow New York to maintain its status as America's top urban center against stiff competition from flourishing cities like Chicago out west. So it was that New York greeted the new century as a giant of a metropolis, encompassing Queens, Kings, Richmond, Brooklyn, and New York counties. Robert Van Wyck, the first mayor of Greater New York, was sworn into office on January 1, 1898.

CHAPTER FIVE

New York Modern

The consolidation of the counties surrounding Manhattan into Greater New York resulted in a metropolis that covered over 300 square miles and in 1900 boasted a population of 3,437, 202: among world cities, only London had more inhabitants. The city now included nearly 600 miles of waterfront and ran on a budget that approached $100 million. With immigrants continuing to pour in from Eastern Europe and Italy, residents felt a need for faster and more comprehensive public transportation. Elevated railroads had crisscrossed the city since the Civil War days, but they were too noisy and too slow to give planners confidence that they were adequate to New York's increasing demand. Electric streetcars had been used in the Bronx and in Brooklyn (dodging them became such a pastime in Brooklyn that they were inspired to name their baseball team the Dodgers), and cable cars had been tried out in Manhattan, but the city's huge population necessitated a means of transit that wouldn't take up valuable space in its streets. Something like London's "Underground" was beginning to look appealing.

Ground was broken for New York's subway on March 24, 1900. Construction proceeded under the direction of John

McDonald and August Belmont II, and took twelve thousand workers four years to complete. On October 27, 1904 Mayor George B. McClellan, son of the Union Civil War general, made a nine-mile trip in twenty-six minutes on an eight-car train running beneath Manhattan. The city's need for the underground system is evident in the numbers of riders the train served in its first days of operation: 110,000 paid the five-cent fare the very first day it opened, and just days later the system was averaging nearly half a million daily riders.

At the turn of the century New York was changing above ground too, as its unprecedented and unsurpassed skyline began to take shape. Bradford Lee Gilbert had built New York's first steel-frame skyscraper, the thirteen-story Tower Building, at 50 Broadway in 1889. When newspaper publisher Joseph Pulitzer unveiled his 16-story *World* building on Park Row in 1890, the competition among New York's builders for a bigger stake of the sky had unofficially begun. The Manhattan Life Insurance Building went up in 1893, and was followed by taller buildings for Standard Oil and American Surety. Nearly as tall and twice as dramatic, the Fuller Building, better known as the Flatiron Building, located at the point where Broadway and Fifth Avenue intersect at 23rd Street, was completed in 1902. Six years later the 47-story, 612-foot-tall Singer Building was constructed at Broadway and Liberty Street; the Singer was the tallest building in the world, but it yielded that distinction just one year later to the 50-story Metropolitan Life Tower, built on Madison Square. The Woolworth Building, a 792-foot tower built by Frank W. Woolworth in 1913 on Broadway across from City Hall Park, managed to maintain its position as the city's, and the world's, tallest skyscraper for a full 20-years.

THEODORE DREISER

It was this New York—widening, deepening, rising—that one of the city's most devoted novelists, Theodore Dreiser, chose for the setting of his masterpiece, *Sister Carrie*, which was published in 1900. For Dreiser, born in 1872 in Terre Haute, Indiana, New York was a place of contrasts, a place in which the richest of the rich commingled with the poorest of the poor and spawned extreme situations of every variety. He came to the city in 1894 and edited *Ev'ry Month*, a magazine he supplied with reflections on the life of the city that fascinated him. Dreiser took his cues from Stephen Crane and William Dean Howells, to whose Central Park apartment Dreiser made a pilgrimage in 1900. He was determined to document the city with an uncompromising realism, and like other Naturalists his writing shows the influence of Herbert Spencer, who had adapted Darwin's theory of natural selection to the social sphere. With this aim in mind, Dreiser based *Sister Carrie* on materials close to hand. Upon his arrival in the city his brother Paul had taken him to visit their sister Emma, who was living with L.A. Hopkins, a fugitive who had stolen over $3,000 from the Chicago tavern where he worked and fled with Emma—leaving job, wife, and city behind—to New York. In Dreiser's novel Emma and L.A. become Carrie and Hurstwood, characters whose paths veer into the opposed extremes of success and failure that Dreiser found so compellingly evident in New York life.

As *Sister Carrie* begins, Carrie and Hurstwood rent a flat on West Seventy-eighth Street. They return money they'd stolen in Chicago—as Emma and her lover had—and Hurstwood invests in a saloon on Warren Street. Carrie learns to appreciate the city under the tutelage of a neighbor, Mrs. Vance: "This woman was the typical New Yorker in many things, some of which were dressiness, jollity, love of metropolitan life, crowds, theaters and gentlemen companions" (Dreiser 320). Hurstwood, by contrast, dislikes New York, particularly because the luxurious life of the privileged elite seems closed off to him: "The walk down Broadway, then as now, was one of the remarkable features of the city. There foregathered, before the matinée and afterwards, not only all the pretty women who love a showy parade, but the men who love to gaze upon and admire them. It was a very imposing procession of pretty faces and fine clothes. Women appeared in their very best hats, shoes, and gloves, and walked arm in arm on their way to the fine shops or theatres strung along from 14th to 34th" (323). His saloon investment fails, and just as James's Townshend in *Washington Square* had plotted a series of moves uptown as he grew wealthier, Hurstwood's financial straits force him to move downtown to Thirteenth Street. His spirit broken, Hurstwood whiles away the hours people-watching in the Broadway Central; meanwhile, Carrie finds work as a chorus line performer. Her success precipitates their separation: she moves into a new apartment and a higher echelon of New York society, taking her $150 per week salary with her. Hurstwood, left to contemplate her success, writ large in the bright lights that advertise her act along Broadway, eventually commits suicide in a Bowery boardinghouse. In Dreiser's view, the stories of wild success in New York were more than counterbalanced by the many, mostly untold, stories of disastrous ruin that Spencer's survival-of-the-fittest doctrine called for and which Hurstwood's decline exemplified.

Coming back to New York as a visiting Londoner in 1904, Henry James, like Dreiser, found the newly expanded, skyscrapered city rather terrifying. As he writes in *The American Scene*, published in 1907: "One has the sense that the monster grows and grows, flinging abroad its loose limbs even as some unmannered young giant at his 'larks,' and that the binding stitches must for every fly further and faster and draw harder; the future complexity of the web, all under the sky and over the sea, becoming thus that of some colossal set of clockworks, some steel-souled machine-room of brandished arms and hammering fists and opening and closing jaws" (*The American Scene* 75). Though James's late prose style is remarkably well suited to conveying the energy of New York in all of its intricacy, James himself feels so overwhelmed that he declares the city beyond the reach of representation in art: "The reflecting surfaces, of the ironic, of the epic order, suspended in the New York atmosphere, have yet to show symptoms of shining out, and the monstrous phenomena themselves, meanwhile, strike me as having, with their immense momentum, got the start, got ahead of, in proper parlance, any possibility of poetic, or dramatic capture" (83). The "monstrous phenomena" James alludes to seem chiefly to have been skyscrapers and immigrants, for he registers a sense of sublime alienation as he meditates upon them. He sees the "multitudinous sky-scrapers" as "extravagant pins in a cushion already overplanted;" the "vast money-making structure" that "overhangs poor old Trinity" seems "quite horribly, quite romantically" to justify itself by "looming through the weather with an insolent cliff-like sublimity" (76, 83). He speaks of the floods of immigrants with a similar horrified astonishment:

> It is a drama that goes on, without a pause, day by day and year by year, this visible act of ingurgitation on the part of our body politic and social, and constituting really an appeal to amazement beyond that of any sword-swallowing or fire-swallowing of the circus. The wonder that one couldn't keep down was the thought that these two or three hours of one's own chance vision of the business were but as a tick or two of the mighty clock, the clock that never, never stops ... I think indeed that the simplest account of the action of Ellis Island on the spirit of any sensitive citizen who may have happened to "look in" is that he comes back from his visit not at all the same person that he went. He has eaten of the tree of knowledge, and the taste will be forever in his mouth. (84–85)

For James, "one's supreme relation," as those of his novels which obsess over the notion of national character demonstrate, is "one's relation to one's country," and the massive influx of immigrants he witnessed on Ellis Island made it possible for him—even as a veteran expatriate—to feel a haunting "sense of dispossession" (85, 86). Terrified and yet entranced, James rendered his impressions of New York in a way that anticipated the response of his modernist heirs to civilization in general, which struck them as similarly alienating, disorderly, monstrous, ruined, and impossible to "capture" without causing art forms themselves to fracture.

Pained though he was by the New York he discovered on his visit, James nevertheless recognized the changing city as a uniquely important source of raw material for the aspiring novelist. When Edith Wharton wrote to James in 1902, he responded by emphatically urging her to explore "the *American Subject*" and to "*Do New York*" (Edel 235–36). The author of *The Valley of Decision*, a novel set in 18th-century Italy, took James's advice, and transformed a lifetime of circulating among New York's moneyed elite into a series of classic novels including *The House of Mirth* (1905), *The Custom of the Country* (1913), and *The Age of Innocence* (1920).

EDITH WHARTON

Edith Newbold Wharton nee Jones was born on January 24, 1862, into a wealthy and prominent New York family with Dutch and English roots. Like the Jameses, the Joneses were steeped in the traditions of European culture, and Edith's education centered on learning languages and mastering high-society decorums modeled on those of the upper classes overseas. In 1885 she married Edward "Teddy" Wharton at Trinity Chapel in the city, and the couple took up residence on a family estate in Newport, Rhode Island. Soon they moved back to New York, where they lived in a house on Madison Avenue, and joined the rest of their social class in perpetuating the routines of Newport summers and European tours. Though her parents had discouraged Wharton's interest in writing while she was young, a breakdown in 1892 provided the impetus to renew her vocation, and some of her poems and stories began to appear in magazines and reviews. With *The House of Mirth*, serialized in *Scribners*, Wharton drew upon the fund of first-hand experiences with which New York society had supplied her, and achieved a huge success, as the novel quickly went on to sell over 100,000 copies.

The novel chronicles the tragic decline of the dazzlingly

beautiful and well-connected Lily Bart from a life of fashion to a life of drudgery and finally to her death from a drug overdose. Addicted to luxury, Lily makes the rounds in New York society while prospecting for a husband wealthy enough to finance her extravagant lifestyle. Accustomed to money, but with her resources dwindling, Lily circulates among the rich as a desirable social accessory (Wharton had originally intended to call the novel *A Moment's Ornament*), helping her rich friends manage their affairs and bring off parties. Eventually, however, she falls prey to the persecution of Bertha Dorset, who slanders Lily as an adulteress so as to draw attention away from her own extramarital affairs. The opening of the novel encapsulates its harsh moral: Lily meets her friend Lawrence Seldon at Grand Central Station and on a whim decides to accept his invitation to have tea in his hotel nearby. The violation of social decorum represented in Lily's unchaperoned visit might seem trivial, but for Wharton, New York is a town of ever vigilant gossips and talkers, a place where even a casual social call can throw the most pristine reputation into a downward spiral. Later in the story, Selden, who claims to believe in a "republic of the spirit"—an idea of freedom "from everything—from money, from poverty, from care and anxiety, from all the material accidents"—provides Lily with a distracting hope of escape from the grim options available to her (*House of Mirth* 108). Ultimately, however, New York society, like Grand Central Station, runs according to a strict code of operations, and the ideal Selden shares with Lily, like the time he shares with her in his apartment, represents a dangerous divergence from that code.

Lily's lack of money, combined with her increasing indifference to rigid social proprieties, make her vulnerable to the hypocritical attack of Dorset, and she is gradually forced into more humble social orbits as Wharton's novel expands to register impressions drawn from the whole spectrum of society. Depressed, dismissed from a position she took at a milliner's shop, Lily dies from an overdose of sedatives. As if to emphasize the cruelty seemingly embodied in the city itself, New York is portrayed under the aspect of happiness only *after* Lily's death: "The next morning rose mild and bright, with a promise of summer in the air. The sunlight slanted joyously down Lily's street, mellowed the blistered house-front, gilded the paintless railings of the door-step, and struck prismatic glories from the panes of her darkened window" (523).

The Custom of the Country, published in 1913, reprises the satirical take on the artificiality of New York high society presented in *The House of Mirth*, but Undine Spragg, the protagonist of *The Custom of the Country* is, aside from her beauty, altogether different from Lily Bart. Whereas Lily evinces a desire for luxury mixed with a sort of latent idealism, Undine is possessed by her greed for wealth and status for their own sake; whereas Lily is tasteful, socially astute, and thoughtful, Undine is uncultured, dull, and capricious; whereas Lily fails to gain the wealthy husband her lavish lifestyle demands, Undine marries into money three separate times. Undine hails from Apex City, Kansas, where her father has made a fortune in business, but the thousand miles or so between Apex City and Gotham don't keep her from dreaming of one day gaining entrée into New York high society: "Even in Apex, Undine's imagination had been nurtured on the feats and gestures of Fifth Avenue. She knew all of New York's golden aristocracy by name, and the lineaments of its most distinguished scions had been made familiar by passionate poring over the daily press" (*Custom of the Country* 28). After the family relocates to the city, she wins the hand of Ralph Marvell, a gentlemanly lawyer and poet whose Washington Square residence and family name signal his connections to the choicest society of old New York. Restless and ambitious, Undine divorces Ralph and marries the marquis Raymond de Chelles, a French aristocrat. She later gives de Chelles up for Elmer Moffet, to whom she had been married before Marvell, and who is now a billionaire art collector. Still, at the novel's end, she is not quite satisfied: "She had everything she wanted, but she still felt, at times, that there were other things she might want if she knew about them" (591).

In its gossip columns and society pages New York begets an image of itself that nourishes an impossible dream of riches and fame in Undine, who is saved the trouble of pursuing it still further only by the scantiness of her information. In effect, *The House of Mirth* and *The Custom of the Country* complement one another, the first presenting the tragedy of its sympathetic heroine's decline, the second presenting the dark comedy of its repellent heroine's success. Taken together, the two novels diagnose a spiritual vacuity concealed beneath the glamour of a society consumed with money-making and status-mongering.

The impact of World War I—which Wharton had confronted first-hand as an expatriate in Paris, where she organized hostels for Belgian and French refugees—made Wharton nostalgic for the New York of her adolescence. She came to feel that the stuffy social order she had critiqued in *The House of Mirth* and *The Custom of the Country* was perhaps preferable, for all the dehumanizing effects of its hollow routines, to the violence and chaos the Great War had put in evidence. She returns to the New York of the early 1870s with a softened perspective in *The Age of Innocence*, published in 1920, just two years after the war ended.

The protagonist of the novel is Newland Archer, a lawyer with an impeccable genealogy who is engaged to May Welland, but who falls in love with May's cousin Ellen Olenska, who is newly returned to New York from Europe, having fled from an unhappy marriage to a rich Polish count. Archer, though perhaps more tolerant of change than his fellow colleagues in the brownstone set, still glories in the order and decorum of old New York, and is capable of relishing even the subtle distinction between the reception accorded a duke who is related to the van der Luydens—New York's reigning family—and one who is not. Newland's love for Ellen triggers a change in his perspective on such niceties of social form, which come to seem only pointless trappings that divide him from Ellen. But when he proposes to her that they go away together, to a place where the "categories" that structure his social world "don't exist," Ellen replies that those who have looked for that place have found that it "wasn't at all different from the old world they'd left, but only rather smaller and dingier and more promiscuous" (*The Age of Innocence* 293). They part company so as to save what they mean to one another. Legible in the couple's renunciation of their romance is Wharton's own renunciation of her former satirical view of old New York's stale order, which seemed to her, from a post-war perspective, at least a bit less small, dingy, and promiscuous than what lay beyond it.

The dawning of modernity prompted writers like Wharton and James to wax nostalgic for older versions of New York. If their geniuses had led them to take more of an interest in New York government than in New York society, however, they would have found perhaps less reason to reminisce, since the same political constellation held sway in the old New York of their youth as in the new New York of their maturity, with Tammany-backed leaders cycling in and out of power, dispensing varied amounts of patronage to the machine, throughout the 1900s and 1910s. Charles Francis Murphy took control of Tammany Hall in 1902 and managed to keep his Democratic Mayor George B. McClellan Jr. in office from 1903 through 1909. In addition to the opening of the subway system, McClellan helped legislate the setting aside of park land, the widening of city streets, and the modernization of the waterfront. McClellan and Murphy made a strong combination: McClellan made sure that Tammany got the kickbacks and government offices it wanted, but reserved the right to appoint competent leaders to the most important positions; Murphy avoided the extravagant excesses of the Tweed years, keeping a low profile so he could collect his millions in graft in peace. McClellan was re-elected in 1905, after a bitter fight between independent candidate and newspaper owner William Randolph Hearst and Murphy. In his second term of office McClellan administered more civic improvements: playgrounds were built, the subway expanded, the water supply ensured by an expansion of the reservoir system, and the Queensboro and

Manhattan bridges completed. Murphy won again against Hearst in 1910, when he succeeded in placing Supreme Court Judge William Gaynor in office as mayor.

Once elected, Gaynor ignored most of Murphy's demands to give back to the machine, and instead worked to purge the city government of graft. Gaynor, who died en route to Europe while reading Emerson's *Essays* in 1913, fostered the growth of culture in the city by seeing The New York Public Library through to its opening on May 23, 1911. Gaynor was succeeded by John Purroy Mitchel, whose term was the first by a candidate not backed by Tammany since the turn of the century. Mitchel's biggest triumph was his effective management of a currency deficiency crisis caused by the outbreak of World War I, but he consistently underestimated the power Tammany wielded and the importance of courting the vote of the middle and lower classes. It was these failings that paved the way for Tammany to retake the mayor's office with Brooklyn County Judge John Francis Hylan in 1917, the same year America entered the war. Under Hylan, New York was able to avoid a near-catastrophe caused by a wartime increase in the use of the city's harbor facilities. New York emerged from the 19 months of America's participation in the war a smooth-running economic giant, poised to enter perhaps its greatest single decade, having replaced London as the hub of international finance.

EARLY MODERNISM

The Armory Show of 1913 marked the arrival of Modernism to America and made New York the nation's center of Modernist activity for ever after. The latest art from Paris, where the cubism of Picasso and Georges Bracques had taken root in the mid-1900s, was available in New York in a small gallery run by Alfred Stieglitz, called "291" after its Fifth Avenue address. Stieglitz, as Ezra Pound said of T.S. Eliot, had "modernized himself," and New York's skyline had acted as a catalyst. Stieglitz took picture upon picture of Daniel H. Burnham's Flat Iron

Building after the skyscraper had prompted him to a vision during a snowstorm: "The Flat Iron impressed me as never before. It appeared to be moving toward me like the bow of a monster ocean steamer—a picture of new America still in the making" (qtd. in Douglas 179). Stieglitz's modern sensibility was evident in the exhibitions he showed at his gallery, which featured the work of Cézanne, Picasso, Brancusi, Matisse, Arthur Dove, John Marin, and Georgia O'Keeffe. But New York was still under the sway of 19th-century tastes, and few people saw these exhibitions. It took the much larger exhibition of the legendary Armory Show to begin turning the city into the capital of modernism it was to become. The massive International Exhibition of Modern Art contained over 1,000 works by European and American Post-Impressionists and Cubists and was held in the Sixty-Ninth Regiment Armory at Lexington Avenue and Twenty-fifth Street.

Though the show was ridiculed in the press, artists sympathetic to the new kind of art displayed in it flocked to the city in the wake of the Armory Show. Modernism in New York gained further momentum when the outbreak of World War I drove a host of French artists to the city, among them Marcel Duchamp, Francis Picabia, Edgar Varése, and Henri-Pierre Roché. Duchamp's famous *Nude Descending a Staircase*, singled out for ridicule by the press among the works at the Armory Show, hung after Duchamp's arrival in the city in the West 67th Street apartment of Walter Conrad Arensberg, a wealthy patron of the arts. In addition to Duchamp, the salon Arensberg hosted included Picabia, Varése, Man Ray, Joseph Stella, and John Covert among visual artists, and William Carlos Williams, Carl Van Vechten, Djuna Barnes, Mina Loy, and Wallace Stevens among writers. Arensberg's and other similar groups in the city allowed the arts to cross-fertilize one another: Stevens's famous "Anecdote of the Jar," for example, which describes the way the placing of a jar on a Tennessee hilltop changes both the jar itself and its surroundings, reflects the influence of Duchamp's "readymades," which he created by selecting ordinary objects—

a bicycle wheel, a porcelain urinal—and presenting them as works of art. The Arensberg circle was the origin of the Dada movement, which spread across the Atlantic to Zurich, Cologne, Berlin, and Paris during the war.

Another sign of the presence of Modernism in New York during the 1910s was the proliferation of "little magazines," the small-circulation reviews and journals that served as forums for avant-garde art and thought: in several cases, little magazines were relocated to New York in order to tap more directly into its emergent modernist energies. The *Dial*, which would later feature T.S. Eliot's *The Wasteland* and boast Marianne Moore as its editor, was founded in 1880 in Chicago, but was moved by manager and editor Martyn Johnson to New York in 1918. *Masses*, a journal launched in 1911 and edited by Max Eastman, was headquartered at 91 Greenwich Avenue, and presented new work by Louis Untermeyer, Carl Sandburg, and Randolph Bourne, among others. Forced to shut down the magazine in 1917 after the Department of Justice charged the editors with conspiracy against the government for its advocacy of resistance to the war, Eastman started the *Liberator*, whose offices were located at 138 West 13th Street, and which published work by Edna St. Vincent Millay, Ernest Hemingway, John Dos Passos, and Elinor Wylie. The *Little Review*, one of the most important and perhaps the most prototypical of the little magazines, was founded in 1914 in Chicago by Margaret Anderson, who moved it to New York just two years later. John Quinn, a prominent New York lawyer, funded the *Little Review*, and Ezra Pound served as one of its editors. Among other important works, it carried portions of James Joyce's *Ulysses* in serial installments in late 1910, and was available in New York bookstores like the Washington Square Bookshop and Brentano's. *Others* was originally headquartered in Grantwood, New Jersey, but founder Alfred Kreymborg moved the magazine's offices in 1915 to Bank Street, where poets like Stevens, Williams, and Moore sometimes gathered.

Nowhere is the promise and excitement of New York's

growing cultural scene captured with more frank exuberance and vividness than in the letters of Hart Crane, who came to the city alone at the age of just 17, from Cleveland, Ohio, in December of 1916. It was the dream of fashioning a writer's life for himself that had brought him to the city, and in his first letter home he is eager to affirm that New York's good medicine is already taking effect: "It is a great shock, but a good tonic, to come down here as I have and view the countless multitudes," he tells his father. Nor is he so dazzled by "the marble facades of the marvelous mansions" on Fifth Avenue, which shine "like crystal in the sun," that he's likely to neglect his work: "Today, and the remainder of the week, I shall devote to serious efforts in my writing. If you will help me to the necessities, I think that within six months I shall be fairly able to stand on my own feet. Work is much easier here where I can concentrate" (Hammer 9). The adolescent gravity with which he expresses his intentions—it's not just "today," but "the remainder of the week" (tacked on for good measure) that he'll spend on his "serious efforts" at writing—is a direct effect of the intensity of Crane's enthusiasm for New York: he simply didn't want his father, C.A. Crane, a businessman who wished that young Hart would pursue poetry as an avocation rather than as a career, to tell him to come home. Much to his credit, Crane did devote himself to his art, an aim he accomplished largely by taking advantage of what the city had to offer: he wrote poems and kept up lively correspondences, struck up friendships with novelists and painters, and got his work published in little magazines like *Others*, the *Little Review*, and the *Pagan*—whose office Crane visited so frequently in search of conversation that publisher Joseph Kling made him assistant editor. After a stint back in Cleveland following his parents' divorce, Crane returned to the city in 1919. His reflections on life in New York in a letter to his friend William Wright, delivered from a perspective less idealistic than that of his first letters, spell out the importance the city had for him: "To one in my situation (N.Y. is a series of exposures intense and rather savage which never would be quite as available in Cleveland etc.) New York handles one roughly but presents also more remedial recess,—more entrancing vistas than any other American location I know of" (Hammer 23). The city supplied Crane with the experiences and scenes that would serve as the *materia poetica* for *White Buildings* and *The Bridge*, the two collections he published before his suicide in 1932, each of which derives its title from one of the "entrancing vistas" only New York could offer in such abundance.

The New York that Crane and others like him sought was centered, increasingly in the later 1910s, in Greenwich Village, a region which in the next decade would come into its reputation as the glamorous and bohemian capital of the Jazz Age. Among its early legends was the young Edna St. Vincent Millay, who came to the city after graduating from Vassar in 1917. Her partying and drinking, her manifold affairs, and her virtuoso poems made her the talk of the town. She lived with her sister on Waverly Place and on Charlton Street, and was involved as an actress and director at the Provincetown Playhouse, where her anti-war play *Aria Da Capo* was performed in 1919. But it is as a poet that Millay, who was the first woman to win the Pulitzer Prize (in 1923 for *The Harp-Weaver and Other Poems*), is chiefly remembered. As the refrain from her justly famous poem "Recuerdo" demonstrates, Millay could convey the heady freedom of life in the Village in just a few simple strokes: "We were very tired, we were very merry—/We had gone back and forth all night on the ferry" (McClatchy 23). In "First Fig" she memorably captures the *carpe diem* spirit that dominated the Roaring Twenties: "My candle burns at both ends;/It will not last the night;/But ah, my foes, and oh, my friends—/It gives a lovely light!" (23). Millay flourished, above all, as the composer of polished, intensely felt sonnets. Her formalism, which contributed to her popularity, serves as a reminder that along with the eye-catching derangement of experiments like Picasso's *Demoiselles d'Avignon* or T.S. Eliot's *Wasteland*, modern art encompassed work done in more traditional styles. Millay's "If I should learn, in some quite casual way," a remarkable sonnet from her first book, *Renascence and Other Poems*, published in 1917, sets a consideration of love and death—the sonnet's traditional themes—against the backdrop of a New York subway:

> If I should learn, in some quite casual way,
>   That you were gone, not to return again—
> Read from the back-page of a paper, say,
>   Held by a neighbor in a subway train,
> How at the corner of this avenue
>   And such a street (so are the papers filled)
> A hurrying man—who happened to be you—
>   At noon today had happened to be killed,
> I should not cry aloud—I could not cry
>   Aloud, or wring my hands in such a place—
> I should but watch the station lights rush by
>   With a more careful interest on my face,
> Or raise my eyes and read with greater care
> Where to store furs and how to treat the hair. (21)

The New York of 1919 comes across in the poem's details—the subway, newspapers filled with news of accidents, the "hurrying man," the "station lights," the advertisements for fur storage and hair treatment. The city itself seems to discourage emotion, since the speaker cannot express grief "in such a place." It fosters instead a practice of indifference that is identified with the soullessness and triviality of the ads for luxuries alluded to in the last line.

MARIANNE MOORE

At the end of the moral spectrum opposite that occupied by Millay was Marianne Moore, whose reputation for reclusion and virtuousness—she famously objected to her protégé Elizabeth Bishop's use of the word "water-closet" in a poem—can make the breathtaking daring and power of her poems a surprise. A longtime Brooklyn resident, Moore's quirkiness made her an icon later in her career: to the public she became an eccentric, proper, angelic old maid who loved zoos, her mother, and baseball. But that image sometimes obscures the fact that she was a brilliant poetic innovator—admired by Ezra Pound, T.S. Eliot, Wallace Stevens, and William Carlos Williams— whose work epitomized the difficulty and eclecticism of the avant garde.

Marianne Moore and Muhammad Ali "Verses" Ernie Terrell

Marianne Moore was to enjoy the "accessibility to experience" New York provided for more than half a century, from her arrival in 1918 until her death in 1972. She was a poet's poet— a favorite of Williams, Stevens, and Eliot—in her first decades as a New Yorker, but by the 1950s, after publishing articles in *Sports Illustrated* and *Life* and winning the National Book Award and the Pulitzer Prize, she became something of a cultural icon. She was asked by Ford to assist in naming a new car (among her suggestions for what eventually became the Edsel were "The Intelligent Whale" and "The Utopian Turtletop"), and she threw the first pitch to open the Yankees' 1968 baseball season. Perhaps the unlikeliest role in which her unlikely renown placed her was that of co-author of "A Poem on the Annihilation of Ernie Terrell" with boxing champion Muhammad Ali.

The meeting took place at Toots Shor's in midtown and was arranged by the late George Plimpton, editor of the *Paris Review*. Ali had no idea who Moore was, and as Plimpton filled him in, he expressed surprise at someone her age going to fights (Ali guessed that she was ninety-six and added tangentially that some "women up in Pakistan... live to be one hundred and sixty" and can still "haul pianos up and down" hills). It was

Moore was born outside of St. Louis in 1887 and went on to major in biology at Bryn Mawr College. She taught at a U.S. Indian School in Carlisle, Pennsylvania, and then moved to Chatham, New Jersey, where she lived with her mother and brother, who was a Presbyterian minister. Her brother became a Navy chaplain in 1917, and the following year Marianne moved

Ali who proposed that they compose a sonnet about his upcoming fight, with each adding lines in turn. Writing on a menu, Ali came up with the first line-and-a-half: "After we defeat Ernie Terrell/He will catch nothing ...," and left it for Moore to supply the obvious rhyme. When she said she was considering "bell," Ali whispered "but hell" to her, which she wrote in; concerned about the rhythm of the line, she changed it to read "he will get nothing, nothing but hell." Moore struggled to come up with more lines, but the pressure to produce poetry on demand inhibited her creativity. Ali took over and finished the poem, which fell four lines short of a sonnet, but which both poets approved:

> After we defeat Ernie Terrell
> He will get nothing, nothing but hell,
> Terrell was big and ugly and tall
> But when he fights me he is sure to fall.
> If he criticize this poem by me and Miss Moore
> To prove he is not the champ she will stop him in four,
> He is claiming to be the real heavyweight champ
> But when the fight starts he will look like a tramp
> He has been talking too much about me and making me sore
> After I am through with him he will not be able to challenge
> Mrs. Moore. (Hall 219–222)

with her mother to an apartment on St. Luke's Place in Greenwich Village and worked at the Hudson Park Branch of the
New York Public Library. Moore had visited Alfred Stieglitz's
"291" gallery in 1915, the same year that her first published
poems appeared alongside new work by Eliot, Pound, Stevens,
and Williams in *Others*. In an interview with Donald Hall published in *A Marianne Moore Reader*, Moore asserted that her
move to New York led her to write more poetry than she would
have written otherwise: "I'm sure it did—seeing what others
wrote, liking this or that. With me it's always some fortuity that
traps me" (*A Marianne Moore Reader* 256). That Moore thought
of the occasion of writing as a fortuitous entrapment—by an
event, a scene, a passage in a newspaper article—is evidence of
her characteristic humility as an artist. In context, her remark
also suggests that New York was important for her not only
because it offered an opportunity for a collegial synergy to come
into play—"seeing what others wrote, liking this or that"—but
also because it seemed to provide her with more fortuities, more
of the chance observations that she would free herself from by
writing poems. She expresses this idea toward the end of an
early poem called "New York":

> It is not the dime-novel exterior,
> Niagara Falls, the calico horses and the war-canoe;
> it is not that "if the fur is not finer than such as one sees
>   others wear,
> one would rather be without it"—
> that estimated in raw meat and berries, we could feed the
>   universe;
> it is not the atmosphere of ingenuity,
> the otter, the beaver, the puma skins
> without shooting-irons or dogs;
> it is not the plunder,
> but "accessibility to experience." (*Complete Poems* 54)

Moore's quotations—almost always set off with inverted

commas and documented, as if her poems were essays, with endnotes—are a sign of her complex relation to the raw materials of poetry. The scrupulousness with which she acknowledged her debts, like the fabled accuracy of her observing eye, speaks to a concern about entitlement. This concern hovers in the background of "New York," in which ideas of art, experience, and "plunder" are woven together with one another in a tangle of implications and coiled ironies. The poem ends with a series of negations that seek to isolate a value to living in New York that isn't tinged with materialism. The last line of "New York," quoted from Henry James, makes the poem a gesture of solidarity with Moore's new Greenwich Village neighbors—the bohemian crowd for whom the swirl of the city's economic energies was less interesting than "accessibility" to the "experience" they would transform into art.

○

CHAPTER SIX

The Jazz Age
and the Great Depression

"Culture," F. Scott Fitzgerald once said, "follows money," and the economic boom that arrived in the wake of the Great War fueled New York's growth during the 1920s, the city's greatest decade. America's involvement in the war lasted just a year and a half, from April of 1917 through November of 1918. The war had crippled the economies of some of the country's chief European competitors, while the economy of the United States, which hadn't been subjected to the costs and damages of war fought on American soil, nor endured them for as long a time, emerged as robust as ever, ready to collect on massive wartime loans to its Allies. In New York, the country's financial hub, the boom encouraged development on all fronts: clubs, theaters, cafés, schools, galleries, magazines, newspapers, publishers, and other institutions and concerns that fostered the production and dissemination of culture flourished during the "Roaring Twenties," causing as extreme a transformation to life in the city as the 20th century was to witness.

At least part of the "roaring" going on in the 1920s in New York derived from the building projects that the postwar boom made possible. Nearly perpetual construction had been the rule

in New York since the mid-1800s, yet even with its unprecedented bridges and skyscrapers in place, the pace of development in the nation's largest city only quickened. The number of
cars on New York streets more than quintupled in the first 10
years after the war, and by the end of the decade there were
more cars in the city than there were in all of Europe. This rapid
increase brought about the construction of several parkways.
The Bronx River, the Hutchinson River, the Saw Mill, and the
Cross County parkways were all built between 1923 and 1931.
The Holland Tunnel was completed in 1927, and the George
Washington Bridge was finished in 1931. The skyline also continued to grow. The Chrysler Building, the Chanin Building,
the Empire State Building, the Daily News Building, the Equi-
table Building, the Strauss Building and the Bank of Manhattan
Trust were all standing by the end of the decade, as were the
McAlpin, Ambassador, and Waldorf-Astoria hotels.

The frenzied energy reflected in the fast-changing landscape
of the city was equally evident in the vigor with which its residents conducted their nightlife. Boom-money fueled the hard
partying that the decade is famous for, and the Prohibition,
which went into effect with the 18th amendment in 1919,
endowed many a gathering with the allure of the forbidden.
Defiance of the Prohibition in New York was a matter of course.
Thousands of arrests during the early 1920s resulted in a mere
17 convictions, and the number of speakeasies in the city at the
time has been estimated to be as high as 100,000. Racketeers
like Big Bill Dwyer, Dutch Schultz, and Frank Costello, who
made fortunes smuggling and distributing liquor, eventually
became powerful enough to influence city politics. Speakeasies
and nightclubs thrived on the exhilaratingly diverse mixture of
gangsters, flappers, artists, Broadway stars, and wealthy high
livers they brought together.

THE HARLEM RENAISSANCE

Postwar prosperity also set the stage for the Harlem Renaissance.
The economic boom made the city an attractive destination for

African Americans seeking to leave the South. The city's economic expansion meant job opportunities, and blacks poured into New York to fill them. In 1890, only one in seventy Manhattanites was black; by 1930, one in every nine. It was during the 1920s that Harlem became the center of African American cultural life in New York, virtually a city within a city. Built up by developers hoping (and failing) to entice Manhattan's swelling class of middle-income whites uptown, the area was eventually opened to blacks, who saw in its nicely laid out avenues and stylish buildings the promise of a higher standard of living than other cities in America could offer them. Better living conditions, together with New York's insatiable appetite for and capacity to present culture, would pave the way for an extraordinary outpouring of creativity by African Americans across the arts, and particularly in music and literature.

At the heart of the Harlem Renaissance was a conviction that combating racial prejudice would best be accomplished by rejecting the approach advocated by Booker T. Washington and adopting instead a more independent, politically radical stance that stressed the importance of cultural achievement over economic gain. The idea, as James Weldon Johnson and others noted, was that artistic accomplishment by blacks in literature, the visual and performing arts, and music would profoundly change the way whites saw blacks, as well as the way blacks saw themselves. The most important organizations devoted to racial uplift—the National Association for the Advancement of Colored People, the Universal Negro Improvement Association, and the National Urban League—were all headquartered in New York City, and though they differed in some of their emphases, they shared a vision of progress through work in the arts. As with Modernism in general, the promotion of African American thought and artwork took place largely in journals, magazines, and newspapers. Probably the most important of these was *The Crisis*, the monthly journal of the N.A.A.C.P., which had been founded in 1910 and was edited by W.E.B. DuBois, author of the influential *The Souls of Black Folk*.

Among the others were the *Messenger*, founded in 1917 and edited by Chandler Owen and A. Philip Randolph, and *Opportunity*, founded in 1923 and edited by Charles S. Johnson. In these magazines the work of writers like Langston Hughes, Countee Cullen, Zora Neal Hurston, Jean Toomer, and Claude McKay was presented for the first time. Reputations made in their pages translated into appearances in magazines aimed at white audiences, such as *Vanity Fair* and *The New Yorker*.

The work of promoting up-and-coming black writers in magazines took place in concert with the work of taking stock of the African American literary tradition. The 1920s saw the appearance of an unprecedented series of anthologies of African American literature, many of which were devoted specifically to poetry. Several of the most notable of these were edited and introduced by James Weldon Johnson, who brought out the *Book of American Negro Poetry* in 1922 and, in collaboration with his brother J. Rosamund Johnson, a two-volume *Book of American Negro Spirituals* in 1925. In 1923 Robert Kerlin, a white professor of literature interested in black culture, published *Negro Poets and Their Poems*. Alain Locke edited an especially influential anthology entitled *The New Negro*, which was published in 1925. The Baptist National Convention published *Gospel Pearls* in 1921 and helped initiate the jazz and blues crazes that swept through New York and the rest of the United States. The anthologies presented the talents of poets like Phillis Wheatley, Paul Laurence Dunbar, and Jupiter Hammon, among others. (Hammon's poetry had appeared in New York all the way back in 1760.) The collections not only helped validate the enterprise of the artists of the Harlem Renaissance by showcasing the successes of predecessors, but put them in position to assume authority that derived from critiquing and borrowing from a tradition of their own.

CLAUDE MCKAY

The poet and novelist Claude McKay was among the first black writers to figure in the Harlem Renaissance. He was born in

1889 in Jamaica and had published two volumes of dialect verse before coming to the United States in 1912 to study at the Tuskegee Institute in Alabama. After a stint at Kansas State College, McKay moved to Harlem and took a position as co-editor of Max Eastman's *Liberator* magazine. He had a reputation as an aggressive advocate of African American progress and independence, mostly as a result of his sonnet "If We Must Die," which had appeared in the *Liberator* in 1919 and urged an active resistance to race violence: "If we must die, let it not be like hogs/Hunted and penned in an inglorious spot ..." (McKay 36). McKay was ambivalent about the promise of Harlem in a way that occasionally links his work to the visions of the modern city voiced by Marianne Moore and T.S. Eliot. In "The Tropics in New York," for example, a vision of New York's plenty— "Bananas ripe and green, and ginger-root,/Cocoa in pods and alligator pears,/And tangerines and mangoes and grape fruit,/Fit for the highest prize at parish fairs"—prompt in the poet a nostalgic longing for "the old, familiar ways" of the Jamaican culture of his youth (31). The poem resonates with Moore's "New York," in which New York's material abundance is marveled over in all its exotic detail, but not celebrated. In "The Desolate City," collected in *Harlem Shadows*, a book of sonnets published in 1922, McKay expresses a disenchantment in terms akin to Eliot's: "My spirit is a pestilential city,/With misery triumphant everywhere,/glutted with baffled hopes and human pity./Strange agonies make quiet lodgement there ..." (52). Though McKay left Harlem in 1922 for the Soviet Union, his later works in prose suggest that uptown Manhattan continued to maintain a hold on his imagination. *Home to Harlem*, published in 1928, captured McKay's conflicted attitude toward Harlem by tracing the exploits of Jake, an army deserter in search of romance on the city streets, and Ray, a Jamaican-born writer who voyages to Europe in search of something beyond the sensuous appeal of Harlem nightlife.

COUNTEE CULLEN

Countee Cullen assumed McKay's mantle as Harlem's most celebrated poet with the publication of his first collection, *Color*, in 1925. Mystery surrounds Cullen's beginnings; he claimed that he had been born in New York City, but some evidence suggests that he was born Countee Porter in 1903 in Louisville, Kentucky, where he grew up without knowing his father or mother. In his teens he was adopted by Frederick A. Cullen, a minister at Salem Methodist Episcopal Church in Harlem. He graduated near the top of his class at DeWitt Clinton High and went on to New York University and Harvard University, where he earned a master's degree in English in 1926. The following year he published his second collection of poetry, *The Ballad of the Brown Girl*, and an anthology entitled *Caroling Dusk*, and came back to Harlem to write a column for Charles Johnson's *Opportunity* magazine. Like McKay, Cullen developed a formal poetic style that contrasted with the jazz-influenced free verse of Langston Hughes. "Heritage," a tour de force in rhymed couplets, asks "What is Africa to me?" and affirms Christian values over those of paganism (Early 104). Evident in the poem, and in much of Cullen's work, is a struggle to speak to and yet transcend the issue of race. The struggle is poignantly presented in Cullen's "Yet Do I Marvel," which concludes "Yet do I marvel at this curious thing:/To make a poet black, and bid him sing!" (79).

LANGSTON HUGHES

In contrast to Cullen, who frequently connected blackness with rejection and pain, Langston Hughes gloried in his racial heritage: "The night is beautiful/So the faces of my people" he sang in "My People" (Hughes 13). He was born in Joplin, Missouri in 1902 and spent his youth in Lawrence, Kansas, and Lincoln, Illinois before going to high school in Cleveland, Ohio. Hughes persuaded his father to send him to Columbia University, but once in the city the plan faded in the wake of Hughes's intoxication with life in Harlem. Hughes's vision and verse were influenced by Walt Whitman, as well as the older poets of the Harlem Renaissance, James Weldon Johnson and Claude McKay in particular. "The Negro Speaks of Rivers," his most famous poem and also one of his earliest, appeared in *The Crisis* in 1921 and brought a commitment to the issue of racial heritage together with an assertion of an expansive, inclusive selfhood reminiscent of Whitman: "I bathed in the Euphrates when dawns were young./I built my hut near the Congo and it lulled me to sleep./I looked upon the Nile and raised the pyramids above it./I heard the singing of the Mississippi when Abe Lincoln went down to New Orleans, and I've seen its muddy bosom turn all golden in the sunset" (4)

Hughes's major poetic innovation was to adapt the forms of jazz and blues to poetry. His first volume of verse, *The Weary Blues*, which appeared from Knopf in 1926, put Hughes's new kind of lyricism on display. The title poem describes the experience of listening to a black musician sing the blues while accompanying himself on a piano: "Down on Lenox Avenue the other night/By the pale dull pallor of an old gas light/He did a lazy sway..../He did a lazy sway...." (33). The speaker is recalling a performance from "the other night," but the repeated lines, which imitate a signature formal feature of the blues, reinforce the sense of the music's power and appeal by hinting that the speaker is still under the song's spell. The musician remains unnamed (though not the street on which the speaker encounters him), and the effect of his anonymity is to suggest that all of Harlem shares in his "weary blues."

Hughes went on to write one of the most vivid and concise summaries of the Harlem Renaissance—the mood of the era, the forces at work within it—in "When the Negro Was in Vogue," a chapter from his autobiography *The Big Sea*, which was published in 1940. It pairs the beginning of "Manhattan's black Renaissance" with the opening of the musical revue *Shuffle Along*, "a honey of a show" which he wryly claims "was the main reason I wanted to go to Columbia" (McLaren 175). Hughes celebrates the era—its theater, its clubs, its singers, its writers—but notes with lament its deterioration under the influence of a dulling commercialism: whites who flocked uptown to take advantage of Harlem's exciting night life "were given the best ringside tables to sit and stare at the Negro customers—like amusing animals in a zoo"; club-owners, "delighted at the flood of white patronage, made the grievous error of barring their own race" from their tables; dancers, singers, and writers tailored their efforts to suit "the downtown tourist trade" (176–77). For Hughes, "Harlem was an unwilling victim of its own vogue":

> I was there. I had a swell time while it lasted. But I thought it wouldn't last long. (I remember the vogue for things Russian, the season the Chauve-Souris first came to town.) For how could a large and enthusiastic number of people be crazy about Negroes forever? But some Harlemites thought the millenium had come. They thought the race problem had at last been solved through Art plus Gladys Bentley. They were sure the New Negro would lead a new life from then on in green pastures of tolerance created by Countee Cullen, Ethel Waters, Claude McKay, Duke Ellington, Bojangles, and Alain Locke. (178)

Hughes "was there" in Harlem during its renaissance and shared in the dream of creating "green pastures of tolerance" along with the other musicians, writers, actors, and thinkers who gave that dream shape and force. The dream that the culture of 1920s Harlem represented for him was not to vanish, but to become, in the suggestive phrase he would employ in some of his well-known later poems, "a dream deferred."

Hughes's path to New York runs roughly parallel to that of another great modern poet who aspired to assimilate aspects of jazz to poetry, Hart Crane. "Let us invent an idiom for the proper transposition of jazz into words! Something clean, sparkling, elusive!" Crane wrote to his new friend, the poet Allen Tate, in May of 1922 (Hammer 86). Just three years

Hughes's senior, Crane, like Hughes, had come to New York from the Midwest—both had spent time in Cleveland, Ohio. Both Hughes and Crane told their parents that they planned on attending Columbia University, and for both the prospect of earning a degree there ebbed as the dream of taking part in the dynamic cultural life going on outside of school in 1920s New York took hold. The "idiom" Crane felt compelled to invent differs from the one Hughes articulated, yet there are moments in the poetry of each that could almost have been written by the other: Crane's "Virginia," for example, begins "O rain at seven,/Pay-check at eleven—/Keep smiling the boss away,/Mary (what are you going to do?)/Gone seven—gone eleven,/And I'm still waiting you...," and Hughes's "Demand" begins "Listen!/Dear dream of utter aliveness—/Touching my body of utter death—/Tell me, O quickly! dream of aliveness,/The flaming source of your bright breath" (Simon 90 and Hughes 96). More than their common interest in jazz, what Hughes and Crane shared was a vision of humanity as a community of the spirit—an ideal both poets saw powerfully expressed in the work of Walt Whitman. Though both were to grow disenchanted with the city, it was in New York that they hoped to see that vision become a reality.

HART CRANE

Harold Hart Crane was born on July 21, 1899, the only child of Clarence and Grace Crane, whose troubled marriage ended in divorce in 1916. He struggled to please both his father, who hoped Hart would go into business, and his mother, who encouraged him to pursue an artistic vocation. Tangled up in his parents' expectations and marital problems, Crane shuttled back and forth between Ohio and New York throughout his young adulthood, working as a clerk in his father's candy business, as a writer of advertising copy, as a poet, and as an editor and reviewer, in accordance with the dictates of quarrels with his parents and his own growing sense of commitment to writing poetry. In 1923 Crane came to New York to stay. After a brief stint with the J. Walter Thompson Agency, Crane, who made friends easily and frequently depended on them for food, money, and shelter, decided to devote himself to his writing. By this time, he had composed and shown to friends—Alfred Stieglitz, Eugene O'Neill, Kenneth Burke, Gorham Munson, Allen Tate, Jean Toomer, and Waldo Frank among them—several of the poems that were to be included in his first collection, *White Buildings*, which appeared in 1926. Several of the most impressive poems of his first book remained to be written—the astonishing "Voyages" sequence of love poems, for instance—but Crane, as he put it in a letter to Gorham Munson in February of 1923, was already "ruminating on a new longish poem under the title of *The Bridge*" (Hammer 123).

Crane admired and envied T.S. Eliot, whose bleak but persuasive vision of modern urban life in such poems as "Preludes," "The Love Song of J. Alfred Prufrock," and his epic *The Waste Land* strongly influenced him. Yet Crane saw Eliot work as a "poetry of negation" and sought, with Whitman as a kind of tutelary spirit, a way of representing the city that would be positive, life-affirming, ecstatic. In Crane's view, Eliot had hit upon the appropriate subject matter of modern poetry, but had failed, in presenting it under the aspect of estrangement, to fulfill the artist's proper function, which Crane imagined as essentially assimilative (Hammer 86). With this project in mind Crane chose New York's Brooklyn Bridge as the dominant symbol for an epic poem that would portray a synthesis of the nation and would also repudiate, by reversing, Eliot's pessimistic perspective on modernity in *The Waste Land*.

Part of the poem's energy derives from the intensity of Crane's response to the landscape and skyline of New York, and though he spent much time elsewhere—Cuba, Mexico, France, California, Ohio—over the nine years during which he wrote *The Bridge*, much of the poem was composed at 110 Columbia Heights in a room he shared for a time with his lover Emil Opffer; the room offered a majestic view of the city and the bridge. Writing to his mother and grandmother in May of 1924

Crane tried to communicate the grandeur of that view: "Every time one looks at the harbor and the NY skyline across the river it is quite different, and the range of atmospheric effects is endless. But at twilight on a foggy evening ... it is beyond description. Gradually the lights in the enormously tall buildings begin to flicker through the mist." He goes on to describe the play of clouds, lights, skyscrapers, and ships in the harbor before turning to the Brooklyn Bridge: "Look far to your left toward Staten Island and there is the statue of Liberty, with that remarkable lamp of hers that makes her seen for miles. And up at the right Brooklyn Bridge, the most superb piece of construction in the modern world, I'm sure, with strings of light crossing it like glowing worms as the Ls and surface cars pass each other going and coming. It is particularly fine to feel the greatest city in the world from enough distance, as I do here, to see its larger proportions" (190).

Seen in its "larger proportions," New York presented Crane with a sublime vision of the strength and promise of modernity he felt the more cynical Eliot lacked the spiritual strength to bring into his poetry. The vista Crane describes in the letter informs the poem with which the epic begins, "Proem: To Brooklyn Bridge." In it Crane presents the goal of the epic quest through American history, geography, and legend that the rest of the poem will elaborate—"to lend a myth to God." Crane is not insensible to the wearying and potentially destructive aspects of life in New York, however, and the poem shifts back and forth in its first half dozen stanzas between these negative qualities and notions of transcendence. The poem opens with the image of a seagull "shedding white rings of tumult building high/Over the chained bay waters Liberty," but this vision of freedom vanishes as the workaday routine of the city takes over and "elevators drop us from our day..." Similarly, a description of the "panoramic sleights" of cinemas, which figure in Crane's view as modern versions of Plato's cave, are placed in contrast to the Brooklyn Bridge, which is addressed directly, "across the harbor, silver-paced/As though the sun took step of thee, yet left/Some motion ever unspent in they stride." The disorienting pace of life among the city's multitudes is figured in the image of an apparently suicidal "bedlamite": "Out of some subway scuttle, cell or loft/A bedlamite speeds to thy parapets,/Tilting there momently, shrill shirt ballooning,/A jest falls from the speechless caravan." In the magnificent concluding stanzas of the poem Crane represents the bridge as a symbol of the integrative power of the imagination: he implores the bridge, possessed of a "swift/Unfractioned idiom," to "sweep" down to "us lowliest" and "of the curveship lend a myth to God" (Simon 43–44).

F. SCOTT FITZGERALD

Like Crane, F. Scott Fitzgerald came to New York from the Midwest, and also like Crane, Fitzgerald came to know intimately the self-destructive tendencies the city of the 1920s, with its fast-paced party life, could set in motion. But Fitzgerald's novels and essays, like Crane's letters, speak eloquently to the allure and promise embodied in the city in something very like the "idiom" Crane proposed to invent to capture the feel of jazz in words—"clean, sparkling, elusive." Fitzgerald might have had Crane's poems in mind when in his classic essay of 1932, "My Lost City," he describes how the vision of the city struck him as he returned to it after a three-year absence: "As the ship glided up the river, the city burst thunderously upon us in the early dusk—the white glacier of lower New York swooping down like a strand of a bridge to rise into uptown New York, a miracle of foamy light suspended by the stars" (*The Crack-Up* 29–30).

Fitzgerald was born in St. Paul, Minnesota, in 1896. He attended Princeton University and served in the armed forces during World War I. He met Zelda Sayre, who would become his wife, while stationed in Montgomery, Alabama. From trips into and through New York during the 1910s, while Fitzgerald was an undergraduate, he developed a taste for the pageantry and drama the city seemed to offer: "I had come only to stare at the show, though the designers of the Woolworth Building and the Chariot Race Sign, the producers of musical comedies and problem plays, could ask for no more appreciative spectator, for I took the style and glitter of New York even above its own valuation. But I had never accepted any of the practically anonymous invitations to debutante balls that turned up in an undergraduate's mail, perhaps because I felt that no actuality could live up to my conception of New York's splendor" (*The Crack-Up* 24). Fitzgerald came to New York to stay in 1919, having gotten truly familiar only with the "New York of undergraduate dissipation, of Bustanoby's, Shanley's, Jack's ..."—a New York he would return to "alas, through many an alcoholic mist"—but itching to take part in its culture and make a name for himself as a writer (24). He rented rooms in the Bronx, on Claremont Avenue, and wrote advertisements for the Barron Collier Agency. His first novel, *The Romantic Egoist*, was rejected by Scribners twice; Fitzgerald quit his job as an adman and returned to St. Paul to rewrite it, where he stayed for six months. Re-titled *This Side of Paradise*, the book was accepted and made Fitzgerald a celebrity overnight: "When I returned six months later the offices of editors and publishers were open to me, impresarios begged plays, the movies panted for screen material. To my bewilderment, I was adopted, not as a Middle Westerner, nor even as a detached observer, but as the arch type of what New York wanted" (26). Encouraged by his success, Zelda welcomed his suit and the two were married in April 1920, just a month after the novel had been published. Fitzgerald's reflections in "My Lost City" provide a glimpse of the luxurious, lively life they led:

> From the confusion of the year 1920 I remember riding on top of a taxi-cab along deserted Fifth Avenue on a hot Sunday night, and a luncheon in the cool Japanese gardens at the Ritz with the wistful Kay Laurel and George Jean Nathan, and writing all night again and again, and paying too much for minute apartments, and buying magnificent but broken-down cars. The first speakeasies had arrived, the

toddle was *passé*, the Montmartre was the smart place to dance and Lillian Tashman's fair hair weaved around the floor among the enliquored college boys. The plays were *Declassé* and *Sacred and Profane Love*, and at the Midnight Frolic you danced elbow to elbow with Marion Davies and perhaps picked out the vivacious Mary Hay in the pony chorus. We thought we were apart from all that; perhaps everyone thinks they are apart from their milieu. We felt like small children in a great bright unexplored barn. (28)

The success of the novel had launched Fitzgerald into a career as an author—his days as an advertising writer were behind him for good. The writing he was doing "all night again and again" was for fashionable periodicals such as *Smart Set, Vanity Fair*, and the *Saturday Evening Post*. As he goes on to say in the essay, "I remember riding in a taxi one afternoon between very tall buildings under a mauve and rosy sky; I began to bawl because I had everything I wanted and knew I would never be so happy again" (28–29).

In *This Side of Paradise* Fitzgerald portrayed New York much like he himself had first seen it, a glamorous city full of romantic possibility; its hero, Amory Blaine, is modeled on the young Fitzgerald. At the end of the novel, however, Amory, who goes to Princeton and then serves as a lieutenant in France, finds himself disillusioned with New York and with life. Like most of Fitzgerald's fiction, the novel portrays both the promise New York seems to symbolize and, after the fashion of naturalist authors like Theodore Dreiser, the betrayal of that promise. His second novel, *The Beautiful and the Damned*, appeared in 1922 and offered a more scathing critique of life among the young, wealthy, nightclub set whose penchants for hedonistic display and extravagant consumption the Fitzgeralds themselves had come to epitomize. The novel traces the rise and fall of a married couple, Anthony and Gloria Patch, whose characters are based on Scott and Zelda. Gradually their lifestyle deteriorates as Anthony falls prey to alcoholism and infidelity. As in Henry James's New York, where social mobility is mapped onto the city's geography, the couple's moral and social degradation is reflected in their move from an apartment on West Fifty-second Street to one on Claremont Avenue—the same street Fitzgerald had lived on while struggling to make a living in advertising.

Fitzgerald gave the enticements and dangers of "Jazz Age" (a term he coined) New York their classic fictional embodiment in his remarkable masterpiece *The Great Gatsby*, published in 1925. Much of the novel takes place on Long Island, to which the Fitzgeralds had moved in the fall of 1922, when the western half of the island was quickly being bought and built up by developers eager to accommodate a growing mass of commuters. The Long Island Express could transport the couple from their home on the north shore of the island, often called the "Gold Coast" because of the wealthy celebrities and business tycoons who built estates there, to the heart of the city in forty-five minutes. Life in the West– and East Egg of the novel is based on life on the "Gold Coast," just as the "valley of ashes" of the novel—the waste land that lies between the residences of the Buchanans, Nick Carraway, and Jay Gatsby, and the city—is probably based on the area known as Flushing Meadow, which in the 1920s became a repository for loads of trash and garbage brought daily by train from Brooklyn.

The novel opens in the spring of 1922 as Nick Carraway, the morally conflicted narrator, moves into a house next to Jay Gatsby's mansion in West Egg. The Midwest Carraway, like Fitzgerald, grew up in had lost its lustre for him after the war and "seemed like the ragged edge of the universe" (*The Great Gatsby* 7). His sole connection in the city is Daisy Buchanan, a distant cousin, who lives a life of luxury with her husband Tom in East Egg, across the bay from Carraway's and Gatsby's residences. Nick becomes fascinated with Gatsby after glimpsing his neighbor standing at the edge of his lawn stretching "his arms toward the dark water in a curious way"—a posture symbolic of Gatsby's gift for hope (25). The novel is in part a record of revelations about the facts of Gatsby's mysterious past, including a relationship with Daisy which he aspires to renew. It is this goal, it turns out, which accounts for his staring across the bay (at Daisy's house), just as it accounts for his fancy car, his beautiful estate, the lavish parties he throws, and most interestingly, his concoction of a glamorous and largely false personal history.

The novel is crisscrossed with trips from Long Island into Manhattan. In the first of these, Nick and Tom stop in the "valley of ashes" to pick up Tom's mistress, Myrtle, wife of used-car salesman George Wilson (27). The three of them convene in an apartment on 158th Street in the city, other guests are invited, and a small party, complete with whiskey, sandwiches and cigarettes, develops; the party ends when Tom breaks Myrtle's nose when she insists she be allowed to refer to Daisy as often as she pleases. Nick's ambivalence about their revelry, and the city in general, is stated explicitly: "I wanted to get out and walk eastward toward the park through the soft twilight ... Yet high over the city our line of yellow windows must have contributed their share of human secrecy to the casual watcher in the darkening streets, and I was him too, looking up and wondering. I was within and without, simultaneously enchanted and repelled by the inexhaustible variety of life" (40). From his position "within and without," the "inexhaustible variety of life" the city seems to present is revealed as a fiction any "casual watcher" might create on the basis of curiosity about goings-on behind the myriad "yellow windows" of the city streets. Nick's perspective reflects that of Fitzgerald, whose fictions articulate both the enchanting and the repellant aspects of life in New York.

The climax of *The Great Gatsby* centers on another visit to the city. Tom, Daisy, Jordan Baker (a friend of Daisy's with whom Nick has a brief fling), Nick, and Gatsby meet in a suite at the Plaza Hotel in an attempt to escape a summer heat wave. While there, Tom confronts Gatsby about his past and his relationship with Daisy, and a bitter argument ensues which Daisy is called upon to decide: she admits to having loved both of them, thus satisfying neither. Unable to bear the unpleasant situation any longer, she begs to go home. Driving Gatsby's car, she accidentally hits and kills Myrtle Wilson, whose husband George later murders Gatsby under the mistaken belief that he was Myrtle's lover and murderer. Nick's decision to head west in the wake of the tragedies serves to link New York to the romantic and ultimately—in the novel's judgement—destructive American dream of success that Gatsby indefatigably pursues.

JOHN DOS PASSOS

In *Manhattan Transfer*, which was published the same year as *Gatsby*, John Dos Passos represented the American dream in more relentlessly tragic terms. Whereas Fitzgerald entertained a sympathy, however qualified, for an idealized, romantic New York, Dos Passos did not: if the city seemed, even from the somewhat disillusioned perspective of the 1930s, to Fitzgerald like a "great bright unexplored barn," it seemed to Dos Passos a "squirrel cage" at the "top of the world," as George Baldwin puts it in *Manhattan Transfer* (Dos Passos 220). Perhaps not surprisingly, Dos Passos and the Fitzgeralds, who had been friends with one another in the early part of the decade, parted ways not long after Scott's success allowed him and Zelda to move to the Gold Coast.

Dos Passos was born in Chicago in 1896, and went on to Choate and to Harvard University. His father hoped that he would go into business, but Dos Passos' interest in politics, nourished by readings in Veblen, Marx, and Max Eastman's *Masses*, led him toward art and radicalism. After graduating from Harvard in 1916, Dos Passos studied architecture in Spain, but following the death of his father a year later, he enlisted with an ambulance unit and served with the Allies in France and Italy until the war's end. He settled in New York upon his return from Europe and published a novel, *The Soldiers*, which appeared in 1921, based on his experiences abroad. In 1922 he moved into Greenwich Village, where he became part of an informal salon that included E.E. Cummings, Esther Andrews, Dawn Powell, and Whittaker Chambers; his circle of New York acquaintances was large and encompassed Theodore Dreiser, Eugene O'Neill, Edna St. Vincent Millay, the Fitzgeralds, and Emma Goldman, among others. Dos Passos was highly ambivalent about New York, and he traveled abroad frequently during the 1920s to distance himself from its materialism. But for the artist in Dos Passos, the city, like the war, presented a source of subject matter that was valuable despite its ugliness, and by 1923 he was planning an ambitious novel about New York. Two years and two trips to Europe later, he finished the novel, entitled *Manhattan Transfer*, while living in Columbia Heights in the same apartment building Hart Crane once occupied.

Published in 1925, *Manhattan Transfer* draws on the techniques of fragmentation and juxtaposition that inform the aesthetics of modern painting and film to portray the dehumanizing forces Dos Passos saw concentrated in New York. Manuscript evidence suggests that he created the novel's several narrative threads separately, then disassembled them and edited them back together in a more abstract ordering: the stories of Jimmy Herf and Ellen Thatcher, the novel's central characters, are picked up and dropped in accordance with broader thematic concerns in order to emphasize the arbitrary machinations of the city itself. Jimmy enters the novel as a child returning to the United States with his mother on an ocean liner during a Fourth of July celebration, a moment that focuses the ideals that his subsequent career in the city will rob him of. Encouraged by his uncle to pursue a job as a banker, Jimmy has an ominous vision of "revolving doors grinding out his years like sausage meat," an image that expresses the threat to his very humanity posed by pursuit of success in the city (120). He later works as a reporter, but grows disillusioned, picturing himself as "nothing but a goddam traveling dictograph" who writes what sells (344). Similarly, Ellen's path through life in the city is plotted so as to bring out the dehumanizing costs of New York-style success.

She makes her way as a dancer, actress, and fashion magazine editor largely by exploiting her looks. She marries Jimmy only because she is pregnant—with the child of Stan Emery, her only true love, who tragically dies young by self-immolation. In one scene, as Ellen dances with Jimmy to help herself forget Stan, she is represented as "an intricate machine of sawtooth steel whitebright bluebright copperbright," with a voice "like a tiny flexible sharp metalsaw" (228). Just as Jimmy becomes a "dictograph," Ellen becomes an "intricate machine" under the harsh demands city life places upon them.

The same year that *The Great Gatsby* and *Manhattan Transfer* were published also saw the founding of one of New York's most prominent and enduring magazines, *The New Yorker*. Led by founder and editor Harold Ross, a legendary stickler for factual accuracy and correct usage, the magazine sought to deliver more in the way of irony and detached observation and less in the way of thought and emotional appeal than most of its competitors. Its stable of star contributors notably included E.B. White, as well as James Thurber and Dorothy Parker, both of whom were part of the fabled Algonquin Round Table. The type of humor that abounded on the pages of *The New Yorker* is mirrored by the sparkling repartee for which the Algonquin group is famous. Along with Parker and Thurber, the Round Table included Robert Benchley, Donald Ogden Stewart, Robert Sherwood, George S. Kaufman, Edna Ferber, Marc Connelly, and Ben Hecht—the city's elite journalists, critics, and dramatists. The group met for lunch regularly between 1919 and 1929, by which time most of them had left New York, as Fitzgerald was to do, for Hollywood. The set's most famous member was Parker. Detectable in her remarkable acid wit are both the delight in aesthetic accomplishment typical of many writers of the era, as well as the harsh sense of disillusionment with which that delight coexisted. In one well-known episode Parker was challenged to use the word "horticulture" in a sentence. "You can lead a whore to culture but you can't make her think," she replied.

The same wit and flair Parker, Thurber, Benchley and the rest traded on in the literary world were the hallmarks of Mayor Jimmy Walker's style in the world of politics. Walker, the "Nightclub Mayor," gave high living New Yorkers a high living leader they could identify with: as Benchley put it, corrupt or not, Walker would probably make "darned good company" (qtd. in Douglas 12). Walker was born in Leroy Street in Greenwich Village in 1881, the son of a Tammany Hall leader and state assemblyman. After high school Walker tried his hand at songwriting in Tin Pan Alley, located on 28th Street between

Repartee at the Round Table

The members of the Algonquin Round Table included some of the most talented writers of the time, but the group is most famous for the quick wit of their conversation.

Novelist Edna Ferber ran into playwright Noël Coward. Both were wearing double-breasted suits. "You almost look like a man," he said to her. "So do you," Ferber retorted.

Raoul Fleischman claimed not to have realized he was a Jew until he was fourteen years old. George Kaufman replied: "That's nothing. I was sixteen before I knew I was a boy."

Dorothy Parker learned that a friend had been injured while visiting London. Parker quipped that the woman must have hurt herself while "sliding down a barrister."

Franklin P. Adams spent a weekend with *New Yorker* editor Harold Ross during which they went tobogganing. What did Ross look like tobogganing, the Round Tablers wanted to know? "Well," Adams began, "you know what he looks like not tobogganing."

A joker patted Marc Connelly's bald head and remarked, "Your head feels just like my wife's behind." Connelly patted his own head. "Why, so it does," he replied. (qtd. in Meade 76, 77, 82, 85)]

Broadway and Sixth Avenue, where several music publishers were headquartered; he scored his only hit in 1905 with "Will You Love Me in December as You Do in May?" With the help of his father Walker gained a position in the state assembly in 1910. Four years later Tammany boss Charles Murphy engineered his move up to the state senate, where Walker continued to gain popularity by sponsoring bills to allow baseball games on Sundays and to legalize boxing. Though Tammany had backed Mayor Hylan through two terms as mayor, the bosses shifted their support in 1924 to Walker, who won handily. Walker practiced a laissez-faire approach to governance, relying on his wit and charm to maintain his good standing with voters. He took 149 days off during his first two and a half years in office, and during the 1929 race, when his opponent Fiorello H. LaGuardia pointed out that Walker's salary had increased by a whopping $15,000, Walker retorted, "That's cheap. Think what it would cost if I worked full-time!" (qtd. in Douglas 12).

Voters became less willing to ignore rumors of Walker's underworld connections and reports of pay-offs and kickbacks when the stock market crashed in October of 1929. The Great Depression hit New York hard: civic improvements stalled, businesses collapsed, and the unemployment rate in the commercial capital of the nation rose to an astonishing 25%. Breadlines lengthened, and Central Park became a clutter of shacks as the number of homeless in the city increased. Samuel Seabury, a former judge and lawyer, led the charge to bring Walker to justice. With the help of New York Governor Franklin D. Roosevelt, Seabury pressured Walker into resigning on September 1, 1932. Though La Guardia had lost to Walker in 1929, a coalition of anti-Tammany independents and Republicans nominated him for the 1933 election, which he won after a vigorous campaign against the two candidates a weak and divided Democratic party put forward.

FIORELLO H. LAGUARDIA

La Guardia presided over the city for three consecutive terms, from 1933 until 1945. He had been born in lower Manhattan in 1882 and then raised in Arizona, where his father, who was in the army, was stationed. The family later moved to Trieste to live with La Guardia's maternal grandparents; still in his teens, he worked as a clerk in the American consulate in Budapest. Fluent in German, Italian, Croatian, Yiddish, French, and Spanish, La Guardia returned to the United States in 1906 and worked as an interpreter on Ellis Island. After graduating from New York University Law School—he attended during evenings—in 1910, he worked briefly as a lawyer before joining the Republican party out of hatred for bossism and was soon elected to a position in Congress. After serving in the Air Force during World War I, La Guardia returned to city politics, and by the election of 1933, had served seven terms as congressman and earned a reputation as an effective, honest, liberal representative of the people.

The economic straits into which the stock market crash had plunged the city clearly called for a different kind of leadership than Walker had given New York, and La Guardia worked hard to improve living conditions in the city. He balanced a $30 million deficit in just one year by instituting a 2% sales tax, cutting back city employees' salaries, and reducing graft. He recruited and appointed genuinely qualified individuals to serve in his administration, regardless of political ties. The most influential of these new officials was Robert Moses, who orchestrated the rehabilitation of Central Park and constructed 60 new parks in the city in his first year working for the city. Moses also oversaw the building of new parkways and bridges: the Henry Hudson, the Grand Central, the Interborough, the Laurelton, and the Belt parkways resulted from his efforts, as well as the Triborough, the Henry Hudson, and the Bronx-Whitestone bridges.

With Moses off and running as parks commissioner, the mayor applied himself to other kinds of improvements. In 1935 he started the first public housing project in the United States with buildings on the Lower East Side and followed with others in Harlem and Williamsburg. He fought organized crime gangster by gangster, slot machine by slot machine. (La Guardia created something of a stir during a photo shoot by taking a sledgehammer to several slot machines himself.) He pushed for the construction in Queens of the North Beach Airport, which was later renamed in his honor. He reorganized the subway system and did away with the elevated railroads, opening the way for further development. It was during La Guardia's tenure that the Rockefeller Center, designed by Raymond Hood and financed by John D. Rockefeller, was constructed. The Center provided New Yorkers and tourists alike with shops, an ice rink, two nightclubs (atop the RCA Building), and two theaters (Radio City Music Hall and the Center Theater). It also provided a much-needed infusion of optimism and pride in the city during the worst years of the Depression.

Though La Guardia and his administration worked assiduously to alleviate the negative effects of the Depression, a high unemployment rate continued to dog New York throughout the 1930s. In spite of the best efforts of City Hall, morale remained low in the city, as it did throughout much of the country—a stark contrast to the high spirits of the previous decade. The carnival of the Jazz Age had come to an abrupt halt, and the literature of New York in the 1930s turned toward the dark, lurid realism of the naturalists to portray the conditions of the times.

NATHANAEL WEST

Nathanael West's novel *Miss Lonelyhearts*, published in 1933, offered an original, sublimely grotesque response to life in Depression-era New York. West was born Nathan Weinstein (he changed his name following the death of his father in 1924) in New York in 1903. He went on to Brown University, where he became friends with classmate S.J. Perelman. After graduating he worked as a manager at the Kenmore Hotel at East Twenty-third Street and then at the Sutton Hotel at East Fifty-sixth, jobs through which he made the acquaintance of writers like Dashiell Hammett and Maxwell Bodenheim. While working at the Sutton, West completed his first novel, *The Dream Life of Balso Snell*, which was published in 1931. The next year he and Perelman, who had married West's sister Laura, bought a farm in Bucks County, Pennsylvania. While living there, West's muse led him back to a 1929 meeting in Greenwich Village with the writer of an advice column for the *Brooklyn Eagle* who thought West's friend Perelman might be able to make something funny out of the bizarre letters she received. The meeting provided West with the inspiration for his masterpiece, which tells of a New York newspaper advice-columnist named "Miss Lonelyhearts" who becomes disastrously entangled in the lives of his correspondents.

Miss Lonelyhearts, who remains otherwise unnamed throughout the novel to brilliant effect, becomes obsessed with the misery of those who write letters to him asking for advice. William Shrike, the feature editor at the New York *Post-Dispatch*, is a kind of Satanic tempter who renews Miss Lonelyhearts' despair by forcing him to confront the pathos of his correspondence afresh, while ironically stressing the impossibility of solving anyone's problems. The novel unfolds in a cartoon-like manner, in a series of fifteen tableaux centering on Miss Lonelyhearts: he takes dictation from Shrike when he cannot answer the day's letters; he gets in a fight at a speakeasy; he argues with his fiancée Betty; he makes a play for Shrike's wife Mary; and so on. In the climactic scene of the novel, Shrike bursts into Miss Lonelyhearts' room and delivers a tirade cataloguing the methods he might use to escape his despair: the satisfactions of farming; the oblivion of a life on an island in the South Seas; immersion in hedonism; and the artist's life. But Shrike's descriptions are send-ups of each of these escapes: "Tell them that you know that your shoes are broken and that there are pimples on your face, yes, and that you have buck teeth and a club foot, but that you don't care, for to-morrow they are playing Beethoven's last quartets in Carnegie Hall and at home you have Shakespeare's plays in one volume." "The church," Shrike says, "is our only hope," but the church, too, is subject to

Shrike's reductive wit, and he dubs it "the First Church of Christ Dentist, where He is worshipped as Preventer of Decay" (West 55).

While the novel deals in matters that clearly range beyond the portrayal of Depression-era New York, the city's wasted landscape forms an important backdrop for the action of the novel as it allows West to imbue the theme of suffering with immediate and local resonance. When Miss Lonelyhearts returns from a trip into the country with Betty, for example, the image of life in the city slums prompts him to recur to his desperate broodings: "When they reached the Bronx slums, Miss Lonelyhearts knew that Betty had failed to cure him and that he had been right when he said that he could never forget the letters." The city's teeming millions overwhelm him: "Crowds of people moved through the street with a dream-like violence. As he looked at their broken hands and torn mouths he was overwhelmed by the desire to help them ..." (62). To provide a setting suitable to the cosmic despair of *Miss Lonelyhearts*, West turned to the infernal "City of Destruction" portrayed by naturalist novelists like Dos Passos, Dreiser, and Stephen Crane.

In *Miss Lonelyhearts* West captured the sense of helplessness and despair that characterized the lives of New York's have-nots during the Depression. Alternately, in his incendiary play *Waiting for Lefty* Clifford Odets captured the willingness to act and righteous anger that many of the city's working poor felt during the period. Based on a New York City taxi strike that occurred in February of 1934, the six scenes of the play elaborate the background situations of cabbies who are debating a strike at a union meeting. In scene one, one of the cabbies, Joe, returns to his apartment to learn that his furniture has been repossessed. His wife Edna is disgusted with Joe's willingness to work for abysmally low wages and urges him to organize a strike. His fear of taking such an action prompts her to remind him of their hardships: not only is their furniture gone, she says, but their children are hungry, need clothes, and suffer from rickets. When she threatens to leave him for an old boyfriend,

Joe agrees that it's time to take action. Each of the subsequent scenes presents a different variation on the theme of injustice and the need to agitate for change, and the play ends back at the union meeting, with the drivers' militant demands for a strike.

The play opened in January 1935 at the Civic Repertory Theater on Fourteenth Street and caused an uproar. Odets ingeniously designed the play's ending to allow the audience watching the play to identify themselves with the audience of cabbies at the union meeting: when the play was performed, the playgoers joined the cabbies in chanting "Strike! Strike!" The strike on which the play is based had clearly come and gone by the time the play was actually performed. The call for a strike, then, which the actors and audience raised together, constitutes a summons to combat social injustice through collective action in a more general sense, across a range of situations and groups. Odets' play is representative of the ideal much of 1930's art strove to achieve: in *Waiting for Lefty* he succeeded in giving a voice, literally, to New York's troubled masses during the heart of the Depression.

CHAPTER SEVEN

New York Intellectuals, New York Painters, New York Poets

On August 14, 1945, half a million New Yorkers jammed into Times Square to celebrate the news that Japan had surrendered and the Second World War had come to an end. As with World War I, New York emerged from the conflict physically unscathed, while European cities—London, Paris, Berlin, Tokyo, and others—had sustained massive damage. As a result, New York's leading position among world cities was firmly reinforced: it was the most powerful city of the most powerful nation on the planet. Horns blared, sirens wailed, and flags waved in Times Square that evening, but the celebrants' joy was not unmixed with a sense of despair. Close to a million of New York's citizens had served in the military forces during wartime, and more than 16,000 of them never came back. Still, at the end of the war the city's strength and visibility were unsurpassed: its economic vitality had returned thanks largely to wartime manufacturing and harbor traffic increases, and its multi-ethnic character had been further reinforced by continuing immigration. For these and other reasons, the newly created United Nations decided to establish its headquarters in the city. The organization accepted the city's proposal for a 17-acre site in eastern

Manhattan on December 11, 1946, and a year later construction of the forty-five glass-curtained stories of the new Secretariat began. In 1947 the English writer J.B. Priestley declared that the New York of 40 years ago "was an American city, but today's glittering cosmopolis belongs to the world, if the world does not belong to it" (qtd. in Oliver Allen 284).

La Guardia, the first New York mayor since Richard Varick to hold the office for twelve years, had announced his retirement in May of 1945. His successor was William O'Dwyer, who had come virtually penniless to New York from Ireland in 1910. He joined the police force, and after earning a law degree, worked his way up the ranks to the position of district attorney of Brooklyn in 1940. He gained notoriety as prosecutor of the crime ring known as "Murder, Incorporated" while managing to maintain favorable relations with Tammany Hall leaders. He won handily over Republican nominee Jonah Goldstein and the No Deal Party's Newbold Morris, and went on to enjoy a popular first term in office. Shortly after he was reelected in 1949, however, rumors circulated of O'Dwyer's connections to underworld leaders like Frank Costello and Albert Anastasia, and the *Brooklyn Eagle* ran a series of ruinous articles describing payoffs accepted by the police department in exchange for protection of gambling operations. Claiming nervous exhaustion, O'Dwyer beat a hasty retreat to Florida from the rising tide of unpleasant attention in New York. He resigned in 1950 after Bronx boss Edward Flynn had persuaded President Truman to name O'Dwyer ambassador to Mexico, where he later opened a law practice.

Former City Council President Vincent Impellitteri served out the remainder of O'Dwyer's unfinished term. He was replaced in turn by Robert F. Wagner, Jr., who presided over the city during a period of great prosperity, from 1954 until 1965. Skyscrapers of the new glass curtain and steel frame variety exemplified by the United Nations building shot up along the length of Manhattan. Lever House, the first of the new glass office towers, was completed in 1952 at Park and 53rd, and others, often featuring open street-level plaza spaces for which a 1961 zoning law provided incentives, followed in quick succession. The dramatic Seagram Building, as well as the Chase Manhattan, Time-Life, and Equitable buildings were among many completed by the end of Wagner's last term.

Upon taking office Wagner had attempted to limit the power of Robert Moses, who simultaneously held positions as parks commissioner and construction coordinator, as well as a seat on the planning commission, but the strong-willed Moses continued to serve the city in all three capacities well into the 60s. During Wagner's administration, Moses oversaw a massive urban renewal campaign, leveling slums and building high-rise apartments throughout the city. Inveterate believer in highways that he was, Moses also continued to write an abstract signature across the map of Greater New York by laying down more expressways. The Cross-Bronx Expressway was only the most controversial (because of the threat it represented to several Bronx neighborhoods) of a group of projects he supervised including the Brooklyn-Queens, the Major Deegan, the Van Wyck, the Bruckner, and the Long Island expressways. The New York of the 1950s resembled nothing so much as the New York of the 1920s, when the city had likewise emerged from a world war with a revitalized economy and gone on a building spree.

As Fitzgerald, Dos Passos, and other Jazz Age writers had shown, though, boom times in New York did not necessarily guarantee happiness or success on an individual basis. In their works good fortune is still subject to critique: it does not come without costs or dangers; a rise is often prelude to a fall; the prosperity of some inevitably accents the poverty of others. The American Dream recreated in 1940s New York is evoked tragically in Arthur Miller's justly famous *Death of a Salesman*, which was first produced in 1949. The play follows the career of salesman Willy Loman, who clings tenaciously to his great expectations only to have them crushed by a business world that cares nothing for his company loyalty and likeable personality.

ARTHUR MILLER

Miller was born on October 15, 1915, to Isadore and Augusta Miller, a well-to-do Jewish couple who lived in Manhattan. Like Biff Loman in *Death of a Salesman*, Miller excelled as an athlete and was handy with tools, but as a student he performed poorly. In 1928 economic conditions forced his father to move the family to a small house at 1350 East 3rd in Brooklyn—the house on which he would model that of the Lomans in *Death of a Salesman*—in a neighborhood that included people from a mix of backgrounds: Jewish, Irish, African, Swedish, and Italian. Miller worked a variety of jobs—dishwasher, singer at a radio station, laboratory attendant, truck driver, factory worker—to help his family during the Depression. Reading Fyodor Dostoevsky's *The Brothers Karamazov* during his daily subway commute convinced him somewhat abruptly that he needed to be a writer. In 1934 Miller enrolled at the University of Michigan and took up journalism. He won the prestigious university-sponsored Avery Hopwood Award with *No Villain*, his first effort at playwriting, which he composed in just four days. After earning his degree in 1938 he returned to Brooklyn and wrote plays for radio programs. He was kept from joining the military by an old injury, but he toured army camps during the war to collect ideas for *The Story of GI Joe*, a movie based on Ernie Pyle's book *Here Is Your War*. He published a journal based on his travels, *Situation Normal*, in 1944. The same year *The Man Who Had All the Luck* was produced on Broadway. He won the New York Drama Critics Circle Award for *All My Sons*, which was produced in 1947. The appearance, two years later, of *Death of a Salesman*—perhaps the best-known play by an American—made Miller a celebrity: honorary degrees, literary awards, money, and, of course, his marriage to movie star Marilyn Monroe, all confirmed his arrival.

In *Death of a Salesman,* New York, like Willy Loman's career in sales, has taken a turn for the worse. The city has been built up, even in the outer boroughs where Willy, his wife Linda, and their two sons, Biff and Happy, live. Its new offices and

apartments ironically mean *less* space for Willy and his aspirations. The Lomans' house is situated so as to emphasize the
encroachment of a bigger, meaner New York upon the family:
"*Before us is the Salesman's house. We are aware of towering,
angular shapes behind it, surrounding it on all sides*" (Miller 11).
Willy underscores this idea early in the play; he asks Linda to
open a window, and when she explains that they're all open
already, he complains: "The way they boxed us in here. Bricks
and windows, windows and bricks." "The street," he goes on to
say, "is lined with cars. There's not a breath of fresh air in the
back yard. They should've had a law against apartment houses.
Remember those two beautiful elm trees out there? When I and
Biff hung the swing between them?" (17). Willy's nostalgia for
an earlier, more pastoral New York parallels his nostalgia for his
past success in sales, which peaked, as Willy reminds his boss
before being fired, in 1928, the same year Arthur Miller's family
was forced to relocate. Biff, high school football star turned
journeyman laborer and kleptomaniac, echoes his father later in
the play: "... we don't belong in this nuthouse of a city! We
should be mixing cement on some open plain, or—or carpen-
ters. A carpenter is allowed to whistle!" (61).

But despite overcrowding and the increase in competition it
suggests, Willy, and Happy after him ("I'm staying right in this
city, and I'm gonna beat this racket!" he declares after his father's
suicide), nevertheless continue to identify New York with success: "I'm gonna knock Howard for a loop, kid. I'll get an
advance, and I'll come home with a New York job" (138, 74).
That Linda echoes Willy shortly after he leaves for his interview
reaffirms the idea: "He may have big news too!" she says glow-
ingly over the phone to Biff, "That's right, a New York job"
(76). Fittingly, it is in Manhattan, at "Frank's Chop House on
Forty-eighth near Sixth Avenue," where the boys meet to treat
their father to dinner, that Willy and Biff share the news that
the prospects both had briefly entertained that day had come to
ruin (74). Believing he's worth more to the family dead than
alive, Willy commits suicide; his funeral, like Jay Gatsby's, is vir-

■ Manhattan, one of the busiest and most vibrant cities in the world, remains at the heart of the American publishing industry. Common points of reference for the city, listed from north to south, are: The Heights and Harlem, Upper West Side, Central Park, Upper East Side, Midtown, The Village, and Lower Manhattan.

■ America's great poet Walt Whitman celebrated New York as "the great place, the heart, the brain, the focus, the no more beyond of the western world." Indeed Whitman spent much of his youth in New York City and taught at New York University.

■ Founded in 1854, McSorley's Old Ale House was made famous first in a series of paintings by John Sloan (1912–1930), and then immortalized in 1940 by Joseph Mitchell's book *McSorley's Wonderful Saloon*. Since its founding, writers such as John Steinbeck have sought out McSorley's, wanting to surround themselves by the history lining its walls and ceilings.

■ In the 1850s Walt Whitman wrote a poem *Crossing the Brooklyn Ferry* in which he unifies Brooklyn and Manhattan under the name "Brooklyniana." Decades later (1883) the Brooklyn Bridge opened; the world's first suspension bridge. Started by John Augustus Roebling and completed by his son, Washington Roebling, the bridge remains as a symbol and heart of America.

■ Born in New York City in 1819, Herman Melville longed for adventure. At eighteen he sailed for Liverpool, beginning a string of overseas travels that inspired his early novels of *South Sea Adventures* and inevitably *Moby-Dick*. He married Elizabeth Shaw in 1847 and returned to New York City for three years before settling in Pittsfield, New York until their deaths when they were buried in Woodlawn Cemetary in the Bronx.

■ Some consider the 21-story Flatiron Building (1901–1903) built by Daniel Burnham to be the city's first skyscraper. Its triangular shape, designed to fit the awkward site produced by the intersection of Broadway and 5th Avenue, became more of a visual spectacle than an economical structure and it drew the attention of O. Henry, P.G. Wodehouse, and countless other writers. To this date, the building, which now houses St. Martin's Press, remains one of the most photographed buildings in New York City and is seen as a symbol of the city's strength and innovation.

■ After F. Scott Fitzgerald married Zelda Sayre, the couple moved to New York City where he wrote his second novel *The Beautiful and the Damned* (1922). No place in his travels showed Fitzgerald the glamour and privilege equal to that found in 1920's New York City. His most well known novel *The Great Gatsby* (1925) is dedicated to that era when the wealthy such as Gatsby lived on Long Island and went to the city for what Nick Carroway remarks to be a "wild promise of all the mystery and the beauty in the world."

■ Dorothy Parker worked at *Vanity Fair* magazine before becoming a founding member of the Algonquin Round Table. She spent much of her time in New York City doing theater reviews and publishing poems and short stories.

■ The Algonquin Hotel was home to the Algonquin Round Table, a social circle of New York wits of the time that met during the 1920s. The Round Table included members such as Robert Benchley, Harpo Marx, Robert W. Sherwood, and George S. Kaufman.

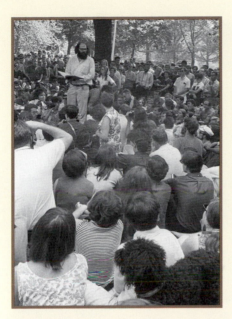

■ The Beat Movement began in New York City in the late 1940s, but was strongest in the 1950s when Allen Ginsberg, William S. Burroughs, and Jack Kerouac became leading figures of the movement In 1966 the New York Supreme Court decided to permit poets to give uncensored readings in public parks, and so figures such as Ginsberg were free to celebrate their more outrageous pieces.

■ Following in the footsteps of the Beat Movement, The Nuyorican Poets Café was founded in 1973 in the living room of writer and poet, Miguel Algarin, as a place where poets and artists could share words and ideas without limitation. When interest burgeoned Algarin rented the Sunshine Café—later christened *The Nuyorican Poets Café*.

■ Opened in 1920 by Frances Steloff, champion of authors and anti-censorship, the Gotham Book Mart has been the heart and soul of the New York literary community. Steloff stocked James Joyce, D.H. Lawrence, and Henry Miller's works when U.S. obscenity laws banned them. She was one of the founding members of the James Joyce Society and the Finnegans Wake Society now gathers at the shop as well. Patrons have included Arthur Miller, James Joyce, Gertrude Stein, E.E. Cummings, Marianne Moore, J.D. Salinger, T.S. Eliot, Thornton Wilder, and Tennessee Williams.

tually unattended. As the characters leave the stage in the final scene, the grim New York of the naturalists rises into view: *"Only the music of the flute is left on the darkening stage as over the house the hard towers of the apartment buildings rise into sharp focus ..."* (139).

The "hard towers of the apartment buildings" emphasized in the stage directions reflect the fact that during World War II and in the two decades or so after it New York was entering a phase of rapid construction brought on by a severe housing shortage. In the 1950s more housing project units were erected in New York than in all the other cities in the United States put together. Between 1940 and 1950 the populations of each of the five boroughs increased by thousands, bringing the city to the highest total population—7,891,957—it would reach before the end of the millenium. The increase was in part the result of the collapse of the economy of Puerto Rico, which sent tremendous numbers of jobless islanders north to New York in search of work: the Puerto Rican population of the city tripled between 1940 and 1950, and nearly tripled again by 1960. Immigrants from Jamaica, Haiti, the Dominican Republic, and Cuba also poured in during the middle decades of the century. In addition, during these years New York saw a rise in its African-American population reminiscent of increases fueled by the Great Migration a quarter-century before. Like many of the newcomers from the West Indies, blacks came to the city hoping to find employment. New York's black population rose from 458,000 in 1940 to 748,000 in 1950 and then doubled over the next two decades.

Race relations had never been simple or smooth in the city, despite some efforts by leaders in the political, social, and cultural realms to improve conditions and reduce discrimination. Circumstances combined to make the years following World War II some of the most strife-ridden and transformational in the history of the city. One of these circumstances was the loss of manufacturing jobs in the 1940s and 1950s: New York's economy had long been driven by its manufacturers, but as the rise of skyscrapers throughout the first half of the century suggests, the city was becoming more and more service-oriented, its millions of feet of office space dedicated to the needs of bankers, advertisers, media professionals, and other white-collar workers. Rising rents and high taxes also stimulated the withdrawal of manufacturers from New York. Factories had traditionally provided newcomers to the city with job opportunities, so their departure spelled trouble for the minorities who were coming to the city in droves. Unemployment left many new arrivals in poverty, which in turn caused conditions in New York's black and Hispanic enclaves to worsen.

The exodus of middle-class whites to the suburbs in the post-war years presents another sign of the escalation of racial tension in New York: 800,000 whites left the city during the 1950s, and another million followed in the 1960s. The poverty of many newly arrived blacks and Hispanics—caused in part by the vanishing of the manufacturing sector—forced them to rely heavily on public assistance. In 1960 blacks and Puerto Ricans comprised a fifth of the city's population, but together they took in three quarters of its welfare payments. Statistics like these, combined with worsening crime and spreading slum conditions in New York's ghettos, generated resentment in whites (who felt the disproportionate flow of public assistance to minorities to be unfair) and frustration in blacks and Hispanics (who were helpless to stop the disappearance of jobs and whose paths to economic improvement were obstructed anyway by all manner of racial discrimination). Riots and demonstrations, many resulting in deaths and arrests as well as legislative change, went on throughout the 1940s and 1950s in New York before climaxing in the 1960s, when the national civil rights movement got fully underway.

RALPH ELLISON

One of the most imaginative and powerful literary works to portray life in New York at this juncture was Ralph Ellison's 1952 novel *Invisible Man*, perhaps the greatest novel written by an American since World War II. Ellison, named after Ralph Waldo Emerson, was born in Oklahoma City on March 1, 1914, and went on in 1933 to study at the Tuskegee Institute, where he focused on music, literature, and painting. Three years later, lack of funds forced him to quit school, and he left for New York. His plans to save money and go back to Tuskegee changed when Ellison met Alain Locke and Langston Hughes on the steps of a library across the street from the 135th Street YMCA where he was staying. Through them Ellison was able to meet his hero, Richard Wright, author of *Native Son*. Ellison had not come to Harlem planning to stay, but under the influence of Hughes, Locke, Wright, and other figures of the Harlem Renaissance, he changed his mind and devoted himself to writing. After publishing short stories and reviews in little magazines during the war and serving briefly as managing editor of *The Negro Quarterly*, Ellison began *Invisible Man* in 1945 while living at 749 St. Nicholas Avenue. As he explains in his 1981 introduction to *Invisible Man*, the novel "continued to preoccupy me in various parts of New York City, including its crowded subways: in a converted 141st Street stable, in a one-room ground-floor apartment on St. Nicholas Avenue and, most unexpectedly, in a suite otherwise occupied by jewelers located on the eighth floor of Number 608 Fifth Avenue" (Ellison vii–viii). The several New York settings in which Ellison composed the novel reflect the multiplicity of viewpoints that inform *Invisible Man*, a work that creatively obsesses over the issue of perspective.

Invisible Man is a semi-autobiographical epic that traces its narrator's journey toward self-knowledge and personal identity. The narrator makes his way north after being expelled—ostensibly only temporarily—from college by its president, Dr. Bledsoe, who is modeled on Booker T. Washington. Like the writers of the Harlem Renaissance, Ellison rejects Washington's strategy of achieving equality gradually through quiet, earnest striving. The narrator is betrayed by Bledsoe, who provides him with what he believes are recommendations for employment, but actually turn out to be letters that warn potential employers not to hire him. He gets a job at Liberty Paints, which ends disastrously: after making a mistake mixing ingredients for "Optic White"—the paint the government uses to whitewash national monuments—the narrator allows a boiler to explode while in a fight with a fellow worker and is then committed to a hospital, where he is used by doctors as a human guinea pig and given shock treatments. After the hospital episode the narrator becomes a spokesperson for a political organization known as the Brotherhood. His success as an orator, however, prompts other members of the Brotherhood to denounce him as an opportunist, and he is demoted from his position as chief spokesperson for Harlem. Ellison covered the Harlem riot of 1943 for the *New York Post*, and *Invisible Man* climaxes with a race riot. Rejecting the communist enterprise of the Brotherhood, as well as the black nationalist cause advocated in the novel by Ras the Exhorter (who renames himself Ras the Destroyer in order to help motivate his audience to rid Harlem of the Brotherhood), the narrator drops into a manhole as the riot rages on. It is from this "hole in the basement" of the city that the narrator addresses the reader directly in the novel's Prologue and Epilogue (7).

The Invisible Man's self-liberation from the ideals and causes through which he attempts to define himself and his role in society occurs as a result of being mistaken for Rinehart, one of the novel's most powerful creations, who, the narrator learns, is not only a preacher, but a numbers runner, a pimp, and a mobster as well: "His world was possibility and he knew it. He was years ahead of me and I was a fool. I must have been crazy and blind. The world in which we lived was without boundaries. A vast seething, hot world of fluidity, and Rine the rascal was at home" (498). Rinehart's protean lifestyle inspires the Invisible Man to practice a new mode of existence that offers the possibility of being "at home" in a chaotic world riddled with paradox and misleading appearances, an alternative conception of selfhood that eschews the foolish consistency that Ellison's namesake, Emerson, called the hobgoblin of little minds: "Not only could you travel upward toward success but you could travel downward as well; up *and* down, in retreat as well as in advance, crabways and crossways and around in a circle, meeting your old selves coming and going and perhaps all at the same time" (510). New York itself also plays a role in precipitating the narrator's realization. On the one hand, its teeming streets bring home the menace of conformity: "The streets were full of hurrying people who walked as though they had been wound up and were directed by some unseen control" (164). On the other hand, as the description of the narrator's first arrival in Harlem suggests, the city's crowds also provide the Invisible Man with an enlarged sense of the social roles blacks might play, and he is shocked to see "black girls behind the counters of the Five and Ten" and white drivers obeying the signals of a black policeman: "And now as I struggled through the lines of people a new world of possibility suggested itself to me faintly, like a small voice that was barely audible in the roar of city sounds" (159). It is precisely this "new world of possibility ... audible in the roar of city sounds" that the narrator comes to see in the example of Rinehart and which sponsors in turn the imaginative freedom he extols in the book's epilogue: "I assign myself no rank or limit ... Step outside the narrow borders of what men call reality and you step into chaos—ask Rinehart, he's a master of it—or imagination" (576).

JAMES BALDWIN
Another writer who captured the enormous complexity of the experience of African Americans in New York in the middle of the century was James Baldwin, who, unlike Ellison, was born and had grown up in the city and whose perspective reflects the deep-rooted familiarity with life in Harlem of an insider or "native son," as he refers to himself in the title of his 1955 book *Notes of a Native Son*. In fact, Baldwin was the first major black writer to be born in Harlem, in August of 1924—the very heart of the Harlem Renaissance. Though he left Harlem at the age of

18, returning intermittently for brief visits, Baldwin continued to draw on the Harlem of his youth throughout his literary career in novels like *Go Tell It on the Mountain* and *Another Country* and collections of essays such as *Notes of a Native Son* and *Nobody Knows My Name*, all of which appeared between 1953 and 1963.

In "Fifth Avenue, Uptown: A Letter from Harlem," an essay collected in *Nobody Knows My Name*, Baldwin returns to where he grew up, an area "bounded by Lenox Avenue on the west, the Harlem River on the east, 135th Street on the north, and 130th Street on the south," to present a view of life along the avenue that "is elsewhere the renowned and elegant Fifth" but uptown turns into "wide, filthy, hostile Fifth Avenue" (Baldwin 170–71). Baldwin aims to critique the innocent, in many ways ignorant, view that "America is still the land of opportunity and that inequalities vanish before the determined will." Not only is the "determined will" rare, he declares, "it is not invariably benevolent" anyway: faith in it goes hand-in-hand with regression to the dog-eat-dog struggling the naturalists deplored by permitting a "disrespect for the pain of others" to flourish quietly (178). The program of self-improvement through willpower resembles the program of urban improvement through renewal because both slight the injustice of racial prejudice: "The people in Harlem know they are living there because white people do not think they are good enough to live anywhere else. No amount of 'improvement' can sweeten this fact" (175). As Baldwin's tableau of an ostensibly revitalized Harlem neighborhood suggests, it would take a great deal more than the "projects" to change conditions uptown: "The projects are hideous, of course, there being a law, apparently respected throughout the world, that popular housing shall be as cheerless as a prison. They are lumped all over Harlem, colorless, bleak, high, and revolting. The wide windows look out on Harlem's invincible and indescribable squalor: the Park Avenue railroad tracks, around which, about forty years ago, the present dark community began; the unrehabilitated houses, bowed down, it would seem, under the great weight of frustration and bitterness they contain; the dark, ominous school-houses from which the child may emerge maimed, blinded, hooked, or enraged for life; and the churches, churches, block upon block of churches, niched in the walls like cannon in the walls of a fortress" (174).

Housing projects were going up all over the city, but the geography of New York in the decades following the war would remain subdivided along racial, religious, and class lines. As Baldwin's essay attests, it was preeminently possible to be *in* New York without being *of* it. In Alfred Kazin's *A Walker in the City*, the first installment in his three-volume autobiography, a visit to New York is depicted as if it were a visit to another country, even though his home in the Brownsville neighborhood of Brooklyn is well within the city limits: "When I was a child I thought we lived at the end of the world. It was the eternity of the subway ride into the city that first gave me this idea. It took a long time getting to 'New York'; it seemed longer getting back. Even the I.R.T. got tired by the time it came to us, and ran up into the open for a breath of air before it got locked into its terminus at New Lots. As the train left the tunnel to rattle along the elevated tracks, I felt I was being jostled on a camel past the last way stations in the desert" (Kazin 8–9).

Kazin, who was born in New York in 1915, was one of the "New York intellectuals"—a group of primarily Jewish writers affiliated with the *Partisan Review* that also included Lionel and Diana Trilling, Irving Howe, Norman Podhoretz, and Philip Rahv, among others. Though feuds within the group were frequent and intense, its members shared a passion for the life of the mind and interest in radical politics, modernism, European culture, and the avant-garde. Howe attempted to define the group in a 1968 *Commentary* essay entitled "The New York Intellectuals, A Chronicle and Critique": "They are, or until recently have been, anti-Communist; they are, or until some time ago were, radicals; they have a fondness for ideological speculation; they write literary criticism with a strong social emphasis; they revel in polemic; they strive self-consciously to be 'brilliant'; and by birth or osmosis, they are Jews" (qtd. in Edmiston and Cirino 255). The contours of their careers reveal other similarities: many of the group's most distinguished representatives grew up in New York's outer boroughs, in squalid ghettos and humble neighborhoods from which they succeeded in escaping through their dedication to writing. Their success in many cases allowed them to take up residence on the Upper West Side where Podhoretz, Howe, and Kazin all eventually came to live.

SAUL BELLOW

The main creative voice of the *Partisan Review* circle was Nobel Prize-winner Saul Bellow, who like Kazin, Howe, Podhoretz, and the other New York intellectuals settled on the Upper West Side. Bellow was born in 1915 in Canada and grew up in Chicago, but like so many writers before him, including fellow Chicagoan Theodore Dreiser, he came to New York to pursue his career as a writer. Philip Rahv recognized Bellow's talent and published several of his stories in the *Partisan* in the early 1940s. After moving to New York, Bellow set his second novel, *The Victim*, which appeared in 1947, in the city. Master of openings, Bellow begins the novel with a striking description: "On some nights New York is as hot as Bangkok. The whole continent seems to have moved from its place and slid nearer the equator, the bitter gray Atlantic to have become green and tropical, and the people, thronging the streets, barbaric fellahin..." (*Novels* 145). Bellow's New York is a city of extremes, chaotic and surreal. He taught in the early 50s at New York University, and lived at 17 Minetta Lane in the Village; later he transferred to 333 Riverside Drive, and subsequent novels, such as *Seize the Day* and *Mr. Sammler's Planet*, are set against the backdrop of the Upper West Side. "New York," as one character in *Mr. Sammler's Planet* declares, "makes one think about the collapse of civilization, about Sodom and Gomorrah, the end of the world" (*Mr. Sammler's Planet* 307–8). Fifteen years of New York was enough for Bellow. His 1970 essay

"New York: World-Famous Impossibility" is hardly a fond farewell: "New York is stirring, insupportable, agitated, ungovernable, demonic. No single individual can judge it adequately. Not even Walt Whitman could today embrace it emotionally; the attempt might capsize him. Those who want to contemplate the phenomenon are well advised to assume a contemplative position elsewhere. Those who wish to *feel* its depth had better be careful. For fifteen years I lived in and with New York. I now reside in Chicago" (*It All Adds Up* 217).

Bellow's view of post-war New York resonates with that of fellow Nobel Laureate and longtime West Side resident Isaac Bashevis Singer, whom Bellow helped introduce to a wider audience by translating his famous story "Gimpel the Fool" from the Yiddish in 1953 for its appearance in the *Partisan Review*. Singer came to the United States from Warsaw, Poland, in 1935, seeking, like the many other Jewish refugees from Hitler who were to change the cultural climate of America during and after the war, to escape the rise of totalitarianism in Europe. Singer's brother, who had come to the States two years before him, helped him get a job with the *Jewish Daily Forward*, where he published book reviews and news features in addition to his fiction, all in Yiddish, for decades after. Singer was an intrepid perambulator and people-watcher: he regularly walked over 100 blocks in a day before going home to his apartment in the Belcord, at Eighty-sixth and Broadway, to write. Aaron, the narrator of his 1968 story "The Cafeteria," possesses a familiarity with the "area that stretches from Ninety-sixth Street to Seventy-second Street and from Central Park to Riverside Drive" much like Singer himself must have had:

> I have been moving around in this neighborhood for over thirty years—as long as I lived in Poland. I know each block, each house. There has been little building here on uptown Broadway in the last decades, and I have the illusion of having put down roots here. I have spoken in most of the

synagogues. They know me in some of the stores and in the
vegetarian restaurants. Women with whom I have had affairs
live on the side streets. Even the pigeons know me; the
moment I come out with a bag of feed, they begin to fly
toward me from blocks away. (Singer 288)

Aaron is a regular at a local cafeteria frequented by Polish and
Russian immigrants. There he meets Esther, a devoted fan of his
writing and a refugee who suffered through imprisonment in
German and Russian camps when she was younger, and the two
become friends. Years pass, the cafeteria in which they met is
burned down and rebuilt, they lose touch with one another for
long periods. One day Esther calls Aaron to arrange a meeting.
There is something she desperately needs to confide in him.
Afraid that he will think her insane, she tells him that she saw
Hitler on Broadway, in the cafeteria, the very same night the
place burned to the ground. Reason forces Aaron to conclude
that she had a vision, "a glimpse back in time": "Even if Hitler is
living and is hiding out in the United States, he is not likely to
meet his cronies at a cafeteria on Broadway. Besides the cafeteria
belongs to a Jew." From then on Aaron avoids Esther, but her
vision prompts him to reflect on his own susceptibility to
insanity: "And what guarantee do I have that the same sort of
thing will not happen to me?" The maddening chaos of New
York itself gives—much as it does in Bellow's fiction—weight to
the narrator's fears of insanity and apocalypse by providing
them with an uncannily likely context: "They are all insane: the
Communists, the Fascists, the preachers of democracy, the
writers, the painters, the clergy, the atheists. Soon technology,
too, will disintegrate. Buildings will collapse, power plants will
stop generating electricity. Generals will drop atomic bombs on
their own populations. Mad revolutionaries will run in the
streets, crying fantastic slogans. I have often thought that it
would begin in New York. This metropolis has all the symptoms
of a mind gone berserk" (297–98).

THE BEATS

The West Side was also the birthplace of the Beat movement, which originated in the mid-1940s in the area around Columbia University, where its central figure, Allen Ginsberg, was enrolled. The "seminal situation," as Ginsberg put it in a 1971 interview, for the movement was the apartment Joan Adams shared with Edie Parker, which was located on 118th Street between Amsterdam Avenue and Morningside Drive. Jack Kerouac, the Beats' most prominent fictional voice, lived there with Parker in 1943; William Burroughs, author of *Naked Lunch*, moved in with Adams in 1944; the next year Ginsberg, who was suspended from Columbia for writing a profanity in the dust on his dorm window, came to stay with the others. "Something happened in Joan Adams's apartment," Ginsberg later recalled, "to all of us" (qtd. in Edmiston and Cirino 264).

It was not in New York but in San Francisco that Ginsberg came of age as a poet: his first book, *Howl and Other Poems* was published there in 1956, and it was there that the obscenity trial for the book took place. Ginsberg lived in San Francisco for most of the 1950s, the heyday of the Beat movement, which despite its New York origins is primarily considered a West Coast phenomenon. Still, Ginsberg returned in 1958 to live in New York, in Greenwich Village, and made the Lower East Side his home for most of the rest of his life. Ginsberg's primary poetic influence was Walt Whitman, and he adopts Whitman's long lines and metonymic style of impressionism in "Mugging," which describes what was becoming an increasingly common experience in New York in the late sixties and early seventies. Its opening catalogues the sights and sounds of his neighborhood: "Tonite I walked out of my red apartment door on East tenth street's dusk—/Walked out of my home ten years, walked out in my honking neighborhood/Tonite at seven walked out past garbage cans chained to concrete anchors/Walked under black painted fire escapes, giant castiron plate covering a hole in the ground/—Crossed the street, traffic lite red, thirteen bus roaring by liquor store...." The thieves make off with $70, some credit cards, and his watch, but leave "my shoulder bag with 10,000 dollars full of poetry." The experience pains Ginsberg, who shares with Whitman a hope for spiritual communion with his fellow citizens, and his disappointment registers in the image with which the poem closes: "'Agh!' upstreet think 'Gee I don't know anybody here ten years lived half block crost Avenue C/and who knows who?'—passing empty apartments, old lady with frayed paper bags/sitting in the tin-boarded doorframe of a dead house" (Ginsberg 625–627).

Ginsberg shared the Village of the 50s, 60s, and 70s with a loosely affiliated group of avant-gardists known as the New York school of poets (a term some critics, and some of the poets themselves, think misleading). Its central figures were John Ashbery, Frank O'Hara, Kenneth Koch, and James Schuyler. Like Ginsberg and the Beats, they were inspired by Whitman. The central place occupied by Zen Buddhism in the poetry of the Beats, however, was occupied by the visual arts in the work of the New York school; Europe, rather than Asia, was their usual destination in travels abroad. The special interest the poets of the New York school took in the visual arts seems natural, in hindsight, considering that in the years after World War II the city was rapidly becoming the new center of the international art scene. Such European luminaries as Fernand Léger, Piet Mondrian, and Jacques Lipchitz made their way to New York in the middle of the century. American painters came to the city too: Jackson Pollock, Lee Krasner, and Willem de Kooning made an important New York debut in a 1942 show organized by the Russian painter John Graham, who exhibited their work alongside canvases by Henri Matisse, Georges Braque, Pierre Bonnard, and Amedeo Modigliani. A later exhibition featured the work of Joseph Cornell and Robert Motherwell alongside that of Jean Arp and Picasso. Pollock, de Kooning, and Motherwell, along with Franz Kline, Barnett Newman, and Arshile Gorky, united by abstract expressionism, also came, like their counterparts in the literary world, to be known as "the New York school."

The stylish new spaces that two of New York's museums came to occupy during the 50s and 60s represent another signal of the city's rising prominence in the art world. In 1959 the Guggenheim Museum, which had been founded in the 1930s with backing from Solomon R. Guggenheim, moved to its current location in a building designed by Frank Lloyd Wright at Fifth and 88th. Similarly, in 1966 the Whitney Museum of American Art moved to its current location in a building on Madison and 75th which was designed by Marcel Breuer. The headquarters of the avant-garde in those years was the Museum of Modern Art (MoMA), the growth of which has made necessary an almost constant process of rebuilding.

FRANK O'HARA

At work in the MoMA in the 1950s and 1960s was Frank O'Hara, champion of the Abstract Expressionists, whose urbane, personal, prosaic verse exemplifies the style most commonly associated with the New York school poets. O'Hara was born June 27, 1926, and grew up in a strict Catholic family in Grafton, Massachusetts. After high school he joined the Navy; he was stationed in San Francisco and then served on a destroyer in the South Pacific. He left the Navy in 1946 and entered Harvard, where he would meet and become friends with John Ashbery during their senior year. He graduated in 1950 and spent a year earning an M.A. at the University of Michigan, where he won a Hopwood Award for his writing. The next year he joined Ashbery in New York, where he worked in the bookstore at MoMA. O'Hara flourished in New York, a city he loved perhaps more than anyone had loved any American city since Whitman had loved it a century before.

O'Hara wrote articles for *Art News* and soon assumed curatorial work at MoMA: after starting with an exhibition of Abstract Expressionist works called *The New American Painting*, he went on to direct or co-direct 19 exhibitions, working his way up the ladder from Administrative Assistant to Associate Curator in just nine years due to his comprehensive knowledge of and inexhaustible passion for postwar art. O'Hara was much more than a scholar of the art he promoted at the museum, he also wrote important interpretations of it, such as his 1959 study *Jackson Pollock*. He was a personal friend and encourager of the painters who produced it, and through collaborations, like the series of lithographs called *Stones* he did with Larry Rivers in the late 1950s, he even took a hand in making some himself. The collections of poetry that O'Hara brought out bear evidence of his participation in the art world. His first book, *A City Winter and Other Poems*, was published in 1952 with drawings by Rivers. *Oranges* appeared a year later with a hand-painted cover by Grace Hartigan. *Odes*, one of his best collections, came out in 1960 and included serigraphs by Mike Goldberg. O'Hara, who lived in apartments at 90 University Place and 441 East 9th Street during the 1950s, turned his apartment at 791 Broadway, where he moved in 1964, into a veritable museum: on the walls hung paintings by Motherwell, Kline, Goldberg, Joan Mitchell, Frankenthaler, and de Kooning, among others.

According to Ashbery, O'Hara's poems speak to "the reader who turns to poetry as a last resort in trying to juggle the contradictory components of modern life into something like a livable space. That space, in Frank O'Hara's case, was not only the space of New York School painting but of New York itself, that kaleidoscopic lumber-room where laws of time and space are altered...". (Donald Allen x) O'Hara's poems take in the New York landscape at, one imagines, a brisk walk, often at midday, which is when he would stroll the streets during his lunch break at the museum: "It's my lunch hour, so I go/for a walk among the hum-colored/cabs," he begins "A Step Away from Them." The "contradictory components of modern life" are brought into stark collage-like juxtaposition in O'Hara's New York, and "A Step Away from Them" turns, with characteristic abruptness, from the pleasurable registering of details to a reflection on the deaths of his friends: "There are several Puerto/Ricans on the avenue today, which/makes it beautiful and warm./First Bunny died, then John Latouche,/then Jackson Pollock. But is the/earth as full as life was full, of them?/And one has eaten and one walks,/past the magazines with nudes/and the posters for BULLFIGHT and/the Manhattan Storage Warehouse,/which they'll soon tear down" (257–58). Here, as in many of O'Hara's poems, New York is emphatically a place of transience: people, magazines, and warehouses alike come and go; their meaning and poignancy inhere solely in their very uniqueness. The theme of impermanence is given powerful expression in O'Hara's most famous poem "The Day Lady Died," in which the day's activities are interrupted—almost too briefly to notice at first—by "a NEW YORK POST with her face on it," which in turn prompts a reminiscence:

> I just stroll into the PARK LANE
> Liquor Store and ask for a bottle of Strega and
> then I go back where I came from to 6th Avenue
> and the tobacconist in the Ziegfeld Theatre and
> casually ask for a carton of Gauloises and a carton
> of Picayunes, and a NEW YORK POST with her face on it
>
> and I am sweating a lot by now and thinking of
> leaning on the john door in the 5 SPOT
> while she whispered a song along the keyboard
> to Mal Waldron and everyone and I stopped breathing.
> (325)

Only art, the poem seems to suggest, can momentarily arrest the ongoing flux that O'Hara identified with life, and particularly life in New York: "everyone and I stopped breathing" at the 5 SPOT precisely because "she whispered a song along the keyboard."

O'Hara's tragic death in 1966—he was hit by a beach buggy on Fire Island at three A.M.—coincides with the end of what New York historian Oliver Allen has called "the last era of good feeling New York would enjoy for some time" (Allen 286).

Mayor Wagner was succeeded by Republican John Lindsay the year O'Hara died. The problems he faced upon taking office only multiplied and worsened during the turbulent second half of the 1960s, though he did manage to keep racial tensions from running to the disastrous levels reached in other cities, such as Detroit, Newark, and Washington D.C., where violent riots resulted in many deaths and severe damages. Lindsay mishandled a twelve-day public transport strike that took place in January of 1966: the walkout cost businesses nearly a billion dollars in losses, which Lindsay then compounded by settling with the union for twice as much as they had originally asked for. Sensing Lindsay's weakness, several other unions quickly followed suit. These settlements took a heavy toll on the city's budget, which was already heavily stressed by a steep increase in the number of New York's welfare recipients. Lindsay's attempt to blame city business leaders for his budget woes resulted only in alienation, as did his attempt to reform the New York Police Department and his feuding with Republican Governor Nelson Rockefeller. In *American Metropolis: A History of New York City*, George J. Lankevich offers a startling summary of the city's troubles under Lindsay:

> Besides the twelve days of the transit strike, Lindsay's first-year experiences included a twenty-five-day newspaper blackout, a thirty-three-day dock strike, and a seventy-five-day hiatus of shipping deliveries. It was a year of unending racial conflict over educational priorities, police-minority relations, and a welfare system whose expenditures had doubled in five years. As if these afflictions were not enough, the city was suffering the effects of a five-year drought which forced restaurants to stop serving water with dinner. Finally, the rate of serious felonies tripled in the 1960s, and "crime in the streets" became a preoccupation of city residents. By 1968, many New Yorkers agreed with the despairing comment by one of Lindsay's trusted commissioners: "The city has begun to die." (205)

NORMAN MAILER

On the scene to chronicle, critique, and help stir up the mayhem of 1960s New York was Norman Mailer, who ran unsuccessfully for mayor of the city at both the beginning and the end of the decade. He was born on January 31, 1923, in Long Branch, New Jersey. Four years later the family moved to Brooklyn, where Mailer grew up and went to high school. After graduating from Harvard in 1943 he was inducted into the army and served overseas for a year and half; it was out of his wartime experiences that he drew the material for his wildly successful debut novel, *The Naked and the Dead*, which appeared in 1948. After a period in Hollywood, Mailer returned to New York and took up residence in the East Village: he got together regularly at the White Horse Tavern at Hudson and 11th streets with Dan Wolf and Ed Fancher, with whom he founded the *Village Voice* in 1955. Mailer went on to live on the Upper East Side, and later established a unique residence in Brooklyn at 142 Columbia Heights, which features a glass pyramid-like gable with which Mailer replaced his roof: that's where his writing carrel is located, on the uppermost of several levels, which are reachable only by using a complex network of ropes, nets, and ladders. In 1959 Mailer published *Advertisements for Myself*, a collection of pieces of unfinished fiction, letters, interviews, journalism, and essays that established him, as *The Naked and the Dead* had not, among critics as a major, if controversial, voice of his generation. The turmoil and scandal of Mailer's life in the 1960s made juicy tabloid material: he stabbed his wife Adele, who was seriously injured, and was committed to a psychiatric institution; he was arrested for repeatedly hailing a police car as if it were a taxi; fought with the officers who arrested him; then defended himself in court and was acquitted; he proposed, during a television interview, that city gangs participate in an annual jousting tournament in Central Park in order to alleviate juvenile delinquency; the list goes on. Yet his outspoken, querulous ways never seemed to obstruct his creative gifts: Mailer closed out the 1960s with the brilliant

Armies of the Night, a nonfiction work for which he won the National Book Award, the Polk Award, and the Pulitzer Prize.

In *An American Dream*, which appeared in 1965, Mailer calls upon the dark vision of the American naturalists who first inspired him in order to come to terms with life in an increasingly brutal, chaotic New York City. The novel recounts the attempt by ex-war hero and professor of existential psychology Stephen Rojack to free himself from the norms of bourgeois society, but to do so without becoming trapped within the harsh conditions of the underworld that lie beneath it. Neither option represents genuine freedom, so Rojack must try to walk a line between them. His murder of his wife Deborah, whom he had married in order to further political ambitions he no longer

Mailer for Mayor

Not content merely to comment on city politics from the sidelines, Norman Mailer twice ran for mayor of New York, both times taking himself seriously enough to force others to confront the prospect of taking him seriously.

The first time, in 1960, Mailer regularly showed up at George Plimpton's apartment in the wee hours of the night, asking him to go campaigning. Allen Ginsberg was recruited to handle the press. His platform was built on the vision of uniting the city's dispossessed—its junkies and hookers and poor—with the cultural elite he was part of. Members of both groups were invited to a party at which he planned to announce his intentions. The night ended disastrously. After a very drunk Mailer, who friends say was battling depression, had challenged many of his guests to fight—Random House editor Jason Epstein, Plimpton, ex-boxer Roger Donoghue, to name a few—he stabbed his wife Adele with a penknife when she reprimanded him for his behavior.

holds, precipitates his fall from respectable society into New York's lower depths, a fall reflected in the geography of the novel, which shifts from the Upper East Side to the Lower East Side and Harlem. In this netherworld he finds love with a cabaret singer, Cherry Melanie, but also violence. After Cherry is pointlessly murdered, Rojack leaves New York for Las Vegas, and thence for the jungles of Central America. Mailer, like Isaac Bashevis Singer in "The Cafeteria," invokes the trope of madness to describe New York: "Sometimes I think there's a buried maniac who runs the mind of the city," Rojack reflects (Mailer 82). For New York City, as for Rojack at this early point in the novel, things would get worse before they got better.

His 1969 campaign turned out much better, though it too was carried out amid a publicity ruckus provoked by Mailer's flamboyance. When Jimmy Breslin, Mailer's running mate, called and brought up the idea of pursuing the offices of mayor and city counsel president, Mailer immediately agreed, asking only that he be given time to go away and lose weight before getting started. "Mailer explained to crowds that he was running on a left-right axis from "free Huey Newton to end fluoridation" (Mills 338–39). The ticket's chances were hampered by the pair's habit of public drunkenness, and by the bad faith of many constituents who had a hard time picturing Mailer behind a desk in City Hall. By the end of the race, Mailer had begun to take himself so seriously that the news—meant to be good—that he had managed not to come in last left him flabbergasted and disappointed. He narrowly beat Jim Scheuer to come in fourth out of five in the Democratic Primary, netting 41,136 votes, just over five percent of ballots cast.

CHAPTER EIGHT

Contemporary
New York

"FORD TO CITY: DROP DEAD" ran the now famous New York *Daily News* headline in October of 1975, the year that the fiscal distress that had been dogging the city since the late 1960s came to a head, and America's most wealthy and powerful metropolis was very nearly forced to default on its financial obligations (qtd. in Oliver Allen 317). The headline refers specifically to President Gerald Ford's obdurate refusal to bail out the city. City leaders, he averred, had created the problem by living beyond their means and cooking the books to cover it up for years, and it was up to them to create a solution. If the city defaulted or went bankrupt for want of federal aid, perhaps the great metropolis, with all its swagger and presumption, would learn a lesson. The numbers city leaders faced on the night of October 16th spelled the lesson out in plain terms: to meet expenses and make payments due the following day they needed nearly $500 million; in the bank, however, was a paltry $34 million.

The city dug into its teachers' pension funds to survive the October 16 crisis, but that didn't solve the larger problem of a massive budget deficit. Mayor Abraham Beame, who had replaced John Lindsay in 1973, had reported the 1975–76 deficit at $641 million, when in fact it was well over $3 billion. Fortunately, Ford and his administrators eventually relented, perhaps because they realized that in teaching New York a lesson in fiscal discipline, they might be shooting themselves in the foot, since the collapse of the country's financial capital could only hurt the national economy as a whole.

The crisis of the mid-1970s was the result of a number of factors. First, the very size and power of the city—home of a fifth of the Fortune 500 companies, more than half of America's 10 largest banks, a third of the country's most prestigious law firms, and just about all of the nation's top advertising agencies—obscured signs of encroaching peril. The 110-story towers of the World Trade Center (they had their own zip code and used enough electricity to light a city the size of Schenectady) had opened in 1972. How could "fiscal disaster" be more than phantom conjured out of political rhetoric in a city that encompassed nearly 30,000 restaurants? The city's massive social services expenditures make up the second reason it flirted with collapse: New York provided more in the way of education, health care, welfare, and public recreation than did many nations, let alone many cities. Chicago, for example, had one public hospital, New York had nineteen. Lastly, there was the issue of the administration's irresponsibility in fiscal matters. Short-term solutions with damaging long-term consequences seemed to be the rule, as Oliver Allen's account suggests:

Finding money became a kind of game, with the most imaginative players praised for their creativity. One year the projected budget was several million dollars in the red, and there appeared to be no further sources of revenue. Whereupon Abraham Beame ... produced a neat answer: he declared the fiscal year to be only 364 days long, so that a big payment due to be made on the 365th day could be ascribed to the following year. Everyone applauded. (311)

With the help of the federal government, which granted the city more than $2 billion in loan guarantees, and by curtailing municipal spending, New York was able to negotiate the economic straits in which nearly a decade of mismanagement had placed it. Unlike Beame's "neat answer," the solution prompted little, if any, applause. Public service jobs were eliminated, and many of those who kept their jobs working for the city had their wages frozen for a period of years. Income taxes increased, as did transit fares; CUNY no longer offered city residents a free education; libraries reduced their hours; day-care centers closed; housing projects were delayed indefinitely. Painful as such changes were to enforce and endure, New York was at least on the road toward stability.

EDWARD KOCH

New York's progress down that road was accelerated by Edward I. Koch, who replaced Beame as mayor in 1977. Beame, who confessed to having lied about city finances, attempted to seek reelection, but Governor Hugh Carey had the Democratic primary delayed so that the SEC report on the causes of the crisis would be published before the election. Carey's blocking strategy worked, as the SEC's investigation proved predictably damning for Beame, whose platform represented a dreamy regression to pre-crisis spending practices: the danger, according to Beame, was far enough behind the city to start upping municipal salaries and putting up buildings. Koch offered a hard-headed alternative to the allure of Beame's siren-song, and New Yorkers went for his no-nonsense, independent style.

Ruthlessly cutting back municipal costs, Koch presided over New York's financial recovery. The number of employees on the city payroll fell by a third between 1975 and 1978 and CUNY pared back its registration by 70,000 students. By taking aggressive measures, Koch was able to turn the city's economy around quickly, and by the end of his first term in office, he was able to start expanding city services again: when he ran for reelection in 1981, he proposed hiring more firefighters and teachers, as well as expanding the police force. He could also boast that city coffers were back in order, as evidenced by the miraculous fact that in 1981, a year before the emergency federal backing program ended, the city reported a budget surplus. As certain as the incumbent's chances for victory in November seemed, however, few anticipated that Koch would win nomination not only from the Democratic, but also the Republican party.

Koch served as mayor for a total of three consecutive terms. Business on Wall Street boomed under Koch during the 1980s, and he managed with relative success the city's move into a post-industrial economic phase: manufacturing jobs continued to decline, but New York's hundreds of banks and brokerage firms grew, and its theaters, colleges, museums, galleries, newspapers and magazines continued to dominate the national cultural scene. But Koch's time in office was not wholly glorious. Wall Street prosperity and balanced books, beneficial as they were to the city, tell only one side of the story. The percentage of New Yorkers living below the poverty line rose by 10 percent between 1975 and 1985. The crime rate rose too, partly as a result of a proliferating drug culture that centered on a deadly new substance, crack cocaine. In addition to these problems, Koch faced administrative scandal. After Queens borough president Donald Manes was found bleeding in a car from a self-inflicted knife wound on Grand Central Parkway, investigators uncovered a network of corrupt city officials, many of whom, like Manes, were Koch's allies, though the mayor himself was never charged. Graft rings, it turned out, infested the city administration, from the Board of Education to the Parking Violations Bureau: a total of 250 officials were convicted before the probe was finished. A year later, just as the hubbub about the scandal was receding, the stock market crashed, destroying the administration's hopes of presenting a rosy economic outlook for the city in 1988. The Koch era came to an end in 1989 as David Dinkins, who would become New York's first mayor of African American descent, won the Democratic primary.

PAUL AUSTER

Paul Auster wrote *The New York Trilogy*—a series of novels that includes *City of Glass, Ghosts,* and *The Locked Room*—in the midst of Koch's reign. Each of the brief, elegantly written novels portrays a bleak, labyrinthine city from which meaning itself seems to have withdrawn. The novels borrow heavily from the conventions of detective fiction, yet to classify them as detective novels feels wrong. They revolve around mistaken identities, impersonation, clues, madness, espionage, and other elements of mystery stories, but their central concerns—language, the self, and the dissolution of both—do not belong solely to hard-boiled literature. As Auster stated in an interview with Joseph Mallia, "I tried to use certain genre conventions to get to another place, another place altogether" (*The Art of Hunger* 261).

Auster was born in Newark, New Jersey, in 1947 and went on to Columbia University, from which he graduated in 1969. He lived in France during the early 1970s, but eventually came back to New York. *City of Glass* was inspired by a series of calls asking for the Pinkerton Agency that Auster received in 1980, while he lived in an apartment in Brooklyn. The novel tries to imagine what might have occurred if he had pretended to be a detective from the Pinkerton Agency. In the novel, a detective-novelist named Quinn receives calls asking for Paul Auster of the Auster Detective Agency; Quinn, impersonating Auster, decides to take the case. The play of identities, even within the first few pages of the novel, is already complex. Auster presents Quinn, who writes under the pseudonym William Wilson about a detective named Max Work, impersonating a detective ironically named Auster. As Auster, Quinn is hired to protect a mad poet named Peter Stillman from his mad father, newly released from a mental hospital, whose name is also Peter Stillman. But "Peter Stillman" might be a pseudonym too, as Stillman himself suggests when he briefs Quinn: "Excuse me. I am Peter Stillman. That is not my real name. Thank you" (*The New York Trilogy* 19).

Tailing Stillman senior takes Quinn all over the city, collecting observations, though his researches only deliver him back into the sense of self-loss that he feels even before he takes the case: "New York was an inexhaustible space, a labyrinth of endless steps, and no matter how far he walked, no matter how well he came to know its neighborhoods and streets, it always left him with the feeling of being lost. Lost, not only in the city, but within himself as well" (4). Stillman's perspective on New York resonates strongly with that of Quinn's, who approaches Stillman one day in Riverside Park and starts a conversation with him. Stillman claims to be developing a new language, one whose words will correspond to parts of a world that has "shattered, collapsed into chaos," rendering current languages inaccurate, obsolete; his method involves collecting broken things on the streets of the city and giving them new names. New York offers Stillman the perfect place to carry out his experiment because it epitomizes with special intensity the chaos that characterizes the fallen world:

> I have come to New York because it is the most forlorn of places, the most abject. The brokenness is everywhere, the disarray is universal. You have only to open your eyes to see it. The broken people, the broken things, the broken thoughts. The whole city is a junk heap. It suits my purpose admirably. I find the streets an endless source of material, an inexhaustible storehouse of shattered things (94).

Stillman may be taken to speak, with a degree of obliquity perhaps, for Auster here, by a sequence of doublings: Stillman is Quinn's double, and Quinn, who takes Auster's name, is Auster's. New York may be a "junk heap," but for Auster it presents "an endless source of material, an inexhaustible storehouse of shattered things."

"These three stories," Auster writes in *The Locked Room*, "are finally the same story, but each one represents a different stage of my awareness of what it is about" (346). *Ghosts* and *The*

Locked Room replay, under slightly different circumstances and with medium-size variations, the plot, themes, and characters of *City of Glass*. In each book the protagonist tails a writer whose actions seem random; he becomes disconcerted by the notion that in following this writer and trying to recreate his thoughts, his identity is dissolving into that of the person he pursues; a crisis occurs and matters are brought to a head in a final confrontation between twin selves. Other details recur throughout the novels, as if by coincidence. "Quinn," for example, is the name of a detective Sophie Fanshawe calls in to search for her husband in *The Locked Room*, setting the stage for an in-joke: "Quinn was no charlatan" the narrator casually opines, though the Quinn from *City of Glass* definitely was (239). Surely this Quinn isn't the same as the one from the earlier novel, but then why, when the narrator of *The Locked Room* thinks he's found Sophie's husband in a bar, does the stranger claim to be Peter Stillman? "My name isn't Fanshawe. It's Stillman. Peter Stillman" (349). The New York of *The New York Trilogy* is an urban chaos so dense with things, people, and actions that, ironically, it becomes impossible to rule out the idea that it is inhabited by some kind of order. Fresh coincidences keep the idea of order alive, but the evidence they offer is never conclusive. The complexity of the city, the paths of Auster's detective-heroes seem to suggest, is analogous to the complexity of the self.

TOM WOLFE

Auster's stark, quiet surrealism contrasts with the rambunctious social satire of Tom Wolfe, whose magnum opus, *The Bonfire of the Vanities*, probes life in "a city boiling over with racial and ethnic hostilities and burning with the itch to Grab It Now" (*The Bonfire of the Vanities* 12). Wolfe was born in 1931 in Richmond, Virginia, and went on to Washington and Lee University for his B.A. and to Yale for his Ph.D. in American Studies. After working for the *Washington Post*, Wolfe joined the *New York Herald-Tribune* in 1962. In the 1960s Wolfe developed the amalgamation of novelistic style and journalistic subject matter that came to be known as the New Journalism. *The Electric Kool-Aid Acid Test*, his 1968 account of novelist Ken Kesey's cross-country trip on a psychedelic school bus driven by Beat hero Neal Cassady, made him a household name. It was late in 1979, at the end of the period he named the "the Me Decade," when Wolfe first began moving on plans he had been kicking around since the 1960s to write a novel about New York; he intended to call it *Vanity Fair* after the 19th-century satire by William Makepeace Thackeray.

Wolfe found it difficult getting started. The novel would be about New York, that much was certain, but what kind of plot would serve the ambitious project best, what characters? Thackeray's novel did not deal with the lower classes, but Wolfe wanted his novel to include representatives from both ends of the social spectrum. To stimulate his creative energies, he watched the goings on at the Manhattan Criminal Court Building, but a friend of Wolfe's told him that to understand what life among New York's poor was really like, he would have to see the Bronx. Only after touring the Bronx, which in the early 1980s was a veritable valley of ashes due to the all but perpetual burning of abandoned buildings, did Wolfe's ideas for the novel begin to coalesce. But after three years of research and note taking, Wolfe still had not written a single scene: in order to force himself to write, he made an agreement with *Rolling Stone* magazine to publish the novel serially, a complete chapter every two weeks. He found writing fiction under the deadline grueling. Second thoughts about characterization and plot worried him. The last serial installment finally appeared in 1985. Wolfe immediately went about expanding and rewriting the story to incorporate changes he had thought up sometimes only hours too late. The revised version of the novel was published two years later.

The Bonfire of the Vanities centers on the gulf between First World and Third World New York: protagonist Sherman McCoy's Manhattan and accident-victim Henry Lamb's Bronx.

McCoy at 38 is a "Master of the Universe" with a Yale degree, a million dollar annual income, and a job with one of Wall Street's top brokerage firms. He lives with his wife and daughter in a massive Park Avenue apartment, which he leaves from time to time for trysts with his beautiful young mistress, Maria Ruskin. But New York, the real New York from which McCoy tries to insulate himself, comes rushing in on him in spite of his best efforts to keep it at bay, turning his life upside down. Driving home from JFK with Maria in his Mercedes, McCoy makes a wrong turn and finds himself lost in the South Bronx: "Utterly empty, a vast open terrain. Block after block—how many?—six? eight? a dozen?—entire blocks of the city without a building left standing.... Here and there were traces of rubble and slag. The earth looked like concrete ..." (82). Trying to find his way back out, McCoy is blocked by a barricade. When he gets out of the car to remove it, two black teenagers approach him in a seemingly threatening way; one of them, Henry Lamb, is hit by the car in the couple's haste to get away.

Lamb goes into a coma, the police trace the car to McCoy, and a host of self-interested New Yorkers rush in to get a piece of the ensuing action. There is Abraham Weiss, Bronx County district attorney and mayoral hopeful, who wants a high-profile case involving a white person in order to rally support from black and Hispanic voters: in McCoy Weiss finds the "Great White Defendant" he has long been searching for. There is Larry Kramer, assistant district attorney, who sees his involvement in the McCoy case as a ticket to higher pay and maybe even a mistress like McCoy's. Representing the media is a tabloid reporter named Peter Fallow who re-energizes his failing career by sensationalizing the story, for which he wins a Pulitzer Prize. New York is no melting pot for Wolfe, who registers in his overdriven mock-heroic style the many ways that New Yorkers differ from one another, from class and race to clothes and cars, and the differences that those differences make in the lives of his characters. If Wolfe's New Yorkers possess a common trait, it would seem to be rapacity. Instead of Ezra Pound's "Make it new," the central precept of modernism, the "motto burned in every heart like myocarditis" in Wolfe's greedy 1980s is "*Make it now!*" (59).

E.L. DOCTOROW
Published contemporaneously with the serial version of Wolfe's *Bonfire of the Vanities*, E.L. Doctorow's semi-autobiographical novel *World's Fair* is set in Depression-era New York and leads up to the World's Fair, which was held in Flushing Meadows, Queens between 1939 and 1941. Edgar Lawrence Doctorow, named after Edgar Allen Poe, was born, like the narrator of *World's Fair*, who is also named Edgar, on Clinton Street in the Lower East Side in 1931. The family moved uptown, and Doctorow graduated from the Bronx High School of Science in 1948. He went on to Kenyon College in Ohio and then to Columbia University, where he studied drama and directing. After a stint in Germany with the Army, Doctorow worked as a reader for film and television companies in New York. In 1959 he was hired as an associate editor at the New American Library publishing company; after five years there he went on to become editor-in-chief at Dial Press. Convinced by his experience as a reader and editor that he was equal to the task of writing a publishable novel, Doctorow wrote *Welcome to Hard Times*, which appeared in 1960. Many of his subsequent novels—*The Book of Daniel, Billy Bathgate, World's Fair, The Waterworks*, and *City of God*—are set in New York, a pattern that seems natural in the work of an author who views Gotham as "the quintessential city," as Doctorow once said in an interview (Morris 202). Growing up in New York offered him a "tremendous advantage": "New York was a very rich experience for a child. As a teenager, I used to go almost weekly to the Museum of Modern Art. I'd look at the permanent collection, look at the new work, go downstairs to the theater and see a foreign film. As a boy I went matter of factly to plays, to concerts. And as I grew up, I was the beneficiary of the incredible energies of European émigrés in every field—all those great minds

hounded out of Europe by Hitler. They brought enormous sophistication to literary criticism, philosophy, science, music.... I was very lucky to be a New Yorker" (201).

In *World's Fair* Doctorow draws on the experience of growing up in New York during the Depression, an historical and cultural moment that contrasts starkly with the decadent and excessive mid-1980s New York in which the novel was published. At the heart of the novel is the vision of the city of the future, as it was represented by the creators of the "Futurama" at the World's Fair. From the perspective of New York in 1985 Doctorow looks back on an older New York, and from that vantage, turns his gaze back toward the present, which he necessarily re-imagines as the "future," with all the idyllic promise and uncertainty that that concept typically implies. Among other effects, this temporal framework allows Doctorow, in returning to the city of his childhood, to do more than duly study the nostalgias: several versions of New York are held in view simultaneously as perspectives confirm, critique, and illuminate one another.

The novel tells of Edgar's coming of age during the 1930s in the Bronx. The extent of the boy's home neighborhood marks the extent of his world, and Doctorow's richly detailed descriptions, drawn and reworked from his own memories, powerfully evoke the atmosphere of the city in the early days of the Depression. Edgar's mother worries over money. His father works in Times Square at the Hippodrome Radio store. Edgar keeps track of New York's three baseball teams, the Giants, about whom he feels indifferently, the Dodgers, whom he considers "Bums," and the Yankees, whom he judges to represent what's best and truest in the city itself: "They were good players who concentrated on what they were doing, who were modest about their tremendous skills and never argued with umpires or played to the crowd. When things were going badly for them, they did not complain but bore down harder. They were civilized and had a naturally assured way about them. That was the true New York quality of spirit" (Doctorow 273). The New York World's

Fair Corporation sponsors an essay contest on the topic of "The Typical American Boy," and Edgar enters. In the opening of the essay, Doctorow brilliantly captures the earnest tone and predictable emphasis on courage that the contest topic solicits: "The typical American boy is not fearful of Danger. He should be able to go out into the country and drink raw milk. Likewise, he should traverse the hills and valleys of the city. If he is Jewish he should say so" (244). The essay wins him honorable mention, which later in the novel allows him to take his family to the Fair for free.

He first attends the Fair with Meg, his friend, and her mother, Norma. Their first stop is the General Motors exhibit, "the most popular in the whole Fair," which features the "World of Tomorrow": "In front of us a whole world lit up, as if we were flying over it, the most fantastic sight I had ever seen, an entire city of the future, with skyscrapers and fourteen-lane highways, real little cars moving on them at different speeds, the center lanes for the higher speeds, the lanes on the edge for the lower. Cars were regulated by radio control, the drivers didn't even do the driving! This miniature world demonstrated how everything was planned, people lived in these modern streamlined curvilinear buildings, each of them accommodating the population of a small town and holding all the things, schools, food, stores, laundries, movies and so on, that they might need, and they wouldn't even have to go outside, just as if 174th Street and all the neighborhood around were packed into one giant building" (252). The note of euphoria is complicated by the multiple perspectives in play here. Surely some of the rapture derives from the sheer massiveness and vibrantly lifelike quality of the display itself, for Edgar already knows what skyscrapers look like, and the highways he knows have cars that move at "different speeds." And from the standpoint of the mid-1980s, well after many older neighborhoods had given way to the huge apartment complexes that Willy Loman deplores in *Death of a Salesman*, it is difficult to share Edgar's excitement at the prospect of "pack[ing]" the neighborhood "into one giant building." It's not that Doctorow is out to discredit the notion of hope by proving Edgar's joy naïve: at the very least, the utopian aspirations made emblematic by the Fair offer evidence that the dream of paradise, one as strongly associated with New York as the nightmare of the inferno, survives and might someday be helpfully revived. But superimposing the vision of the Fair on an image of the New York of the mid-1980s yields a range of gloomy resonances that carry more force for being mixed into the peppy flow of Edgar's impressions: "Meg tugged my arm. 'Look, Edgar!' We were going past what I had thought was only another building. But on the roof was a truly amazing sight, a gigantic red revolving National Cash Register, seven stories high. It showed the day's Fair attendance as if it were ringing up sales. Clouds floated peacefully behind it" (256).

OSCAR HIJUELOS

Like Doctorow, novelist Oscar Hijuelos returned to the New York of his youth in *The Mambo Kings Play Songs of Love*, which was published in 1989 and won the Pulitzer Prize. Hijuelos was born in 1951 in New York. His parents had immigrated to the United States in 1943 and settled in Spanish Harlem, where Hijuelos grew up. He played guitar in various pop bands as a teenager in the 1960s, and his first-hand experience in the music scene helps to endow his evocation of New York in the mambo-mad 1950s with a great richness of detail and insight. He went on to City College, from which he graduated with a bachelor's degree in 1975, and where he stayed to take a master's degree in creative writing a year later. He worked for Transportation Display, Inc., an advertising firm, for seven years while continuing to pursue writing during his off-hours. His first novel, *Our House in the Last World*, appeared in 1985 to wide acclaim.

Much like *World's Fair*, Hijuelos's novel presents a lushly described portrait of New York on the other side of the tumultuous cultural changes of the late 1960s. The novel chronicles the fortunes of the Castillo brothers, Nestor and Cesar, who leave Havana for New York in 1949. Together with other musicians they form a mambo band called the Mambo Kings just as the craze for such orchestras was beginning to spread through the dance halls. "Working in a meat-packing plant on 125th Street by day so that they could have enough money to party and set things up at night," the brothers attract the notice of Desi Arnaz, a bandleader and television personality, who lands them an appearance on the *I Love Lucy* show as Ricky Ricardo's singing cousins (Hijuelos 21). During the episode they perform "Beautiful Maria of My Soul," which becomes a hit, and for a brief time they enjoy a status as minor celebrities, though life in the fast lane takes its toll, and their appearance on *I Love Lucy* assumes its position as the brief but oft-cherished high point of their lives.

Nostalgia is represented in several forms in the novel, not the least important of which is the complex nostalgia of the brothers for the Cuba they left behind. Nestor, who marries in the States, remains burdened by the memory of his unrequited love for Maria, whom he knew in Cuba, and whose memory inspires the Mambo Kings' hit tune. Cesar, endless pursuer of women, has left behind a wife as well as a daughter. This was a time "when every Cuban in New York knew every other Cuban," and the novel compellingly portrays the life of the immigrant community and the kinds of ambivalence that can attend the process of cultural assimilation (126). In addition, the novel is pervaded by a deep nostalgia for 1950s New York, which is recalled from the perspective of the New York of 1980, a year that finds the "Mambo King" a disappointed alcoholic holed up in the Hotel Splendour:

> Everything was different then: 125th Street was jumping with clubs, there was less violence, there were fewer beggars, more mutual respect between people; he [Cesar] could take a late-night stroll from the apartment on La Salle Street, head down Broadway, cut east on 110th Street to Central Park, and then walk along its twisting paths and across the

little bridges and over streams and rocks, enjoying the scent of the woods and nature's beauty without worry. He'd make his way to the Park Palace Ballroom on East 110th Street to hear Machito or Tito Puente, find musician friends at the bar, chase women, dance. Back then, you could walk through that park wearing your best clothes and a nice expensive watch without someone coming up behind you and pressing a knife against your neck. Man, those days are gone forever. (11)

New York in "those days" was a modest paradise, and in order to represent it this description, like others in the literary history of the city, mingles the urban with the pastoral, New York's streets and clubs with its streams, rocks, and woods. The difference that is most emphasized, perhaps not surprisingly considering New York's increasing crime rate in the 1970s and 1980s, is a difference in the level of respect New Yorkers accord one another.

TONY KUSHER
The increase in street crime was not the only crisis the city confronted in the 1980s. The AIDS epidemic hit New York especially hard, particularly during the mid-1980s, when a quarter of all the cases of the syndrome in America were reported in New York. "It's 1986 and there's a *plague*, half my friends are dead and I'm only thirty-one," exclaims Prior Walter, protagonist of Tony Kushner's *Angels in America*, which was hailed by many critics as the most profoundly imaginative, searching American play of its time (*Perestroika* 47). Composed of two parts, *Millenium Approaches* and *Perestroika*, *Angels* presents "A Gay Fantasia on National Themes," using the experiences of two AIDS-sufferers to focus an exploration of a range of subjects and issues, public and private, from love to politics to God's abandonment of the cosmos. Parts of the play are set in Washington, the Bronx, Salt Lake City, and Antarctica, but most of it takes place in New York, the American setting of

choice for representing apocalypse, change in the world order, the onset of the new millenium, and related visions. As Harper Pitt declares as she stands at the railing of the Promenade in Brooklyn Heights: "Nothing like storm clouds over Manhattan to get you in the mood for Judgment Day" (*Perestroika* 99).

Kushner, whom his parents, both musicians, named after singer Tony Bennet, was born in New York on July 16, 1956. He spent most of his childhood in Lake Charles, Louisiana, where he first got interested in theater as a result of his mother's involvement as an amateur actress in local plays. In 1974 Kushner came back to New York to begin at Columbia University, from which he graduated four years later with a degree in English. He was entranced by the New York theater scene and he frequently went to shows on Broadway as well as at the city's many smaller performance venues. In the years following his graduation from Columbia, Kushner struggled with his sexual orientation, and even tried to "cure" his homosexuality through therapy. In 1981 he called his mother from a phone booth in New York to tell her he was gay, a moment he would recreate years later in *Angels*, in the scene in which Joe Pitt, a married Mormon lawyer, calls his mother in Salt Lake City in the middle of the night: "I'm a homosexual, Momma. Boy, did that come out awkward," he says, "We will just forget this phone call," she responds (*Millenium Approaches* 75–76). He worked as a switchboard operator at the United Nations Plaza Hotel for a few years before enrolling in New York University's Tisch School of the Arts to pursue a degree in directing. By the time Kushner started composing *Angels*, he had written a number of plays spanning a wide range of styles and genres—an opera, several plays for children's theater, one-acts and full-length dramas. Oskar Eustis, the artistic director of the Eureka Theater in San Francisco, commissioned Kushner to write *Angels* on the basis of Kushner's *A Bright Room Called Day*, which premiered in 1987: it follows the disintegration of a group of friends during Hitler's rise to power and draws parallels between the Nazi regime and the Reagan administration.

Millenium Approaches, the first part of *Angels*, was first presented by the Center Theatre Group at Mark Taper Forum in
May of 1990. Most of the action of *Angels* revolves around two
couples: Joe and Harper Pitt, a married twosome, and Prior
Walter and Louis Ironson, a gay pair. Harper is an agoraphobic
valium addict who is beginning to feel out of touch with her
husband Joe. Her concerns stem largely from Joe's growing
awareness of his homosexuality, and he later forms an unlikely
sexual relationship with Louis, with whom he works at the
Second Circuit Federal Court of appeals, and whose liberal politics conflict with Joe's, which are rooted in his Mormon beliefs.
Louis falls into a relationship with Joe because he has abandoned Prior Walter, who is HIV-positive and has shown Louis
his first lesion: "Lesion number one. Lookit. The wine-dark kiss
of the angel of death" (*Millenium* 21). Joe works for Roy Cohn,
a character based on a real-life attorney of the same name. Cohn
the historical figure first became famous for securing the death
penalty for Julius and Ethel Rosenberg and later shared the
limelight with Senator Joe McCarthy as they worked together
on hunting down communists during the witch hunts of the
early 1950s. Cohn the demonic character is one of the play's
greatest inventions, and Kushner uses the historical Cohn's
aggressively anti-homosexual political stance and death from
AIDS in 1986 to explore issues relating to closeted gays in positions of power. When Henry, Cohn's doctor, tells him he has
AIDS, Cohn resists, telling Henry that he's hung up on language: "Homosexual. Gay. Lesbian. You think these are names
that tell you who someone sleeps with, but they don't tell you
that." Henry responds with a confused "No?" and Roy tries to
set him straight with his usual verbal gusto:

> Like all labels they tell you one thing and one thing only:
> where does an individual so identified fit in the food chain,
> the pecking order? Not ideology, or sexual taste, but some-
> thing much simpler: clout ... Now to someone who does not
> understand this, homosexual is what I am because I have sex

with men. But really this is wrong. Homosexuals are not men who sleep with other men. Homosexuals are men who in fifteen years of trying cannot get a pissant antidiscrimination bill through City Council. Homosexuals are men who know nobody and who nobody knows. Who have zero clout. Does this sound like me, Henry? (45)

Of course the question is rhetorical; Roy, as he himself goes on to explain, can get the President's wife on the phone in five minutes.

As Roy and Prior stand poised on the brink of death, the characters' lives become more deeply entangled. More questions about love, sex, politics, loyalty, and friendship begin to emerge, a process of development that is quickened and enhanced by the play's mutual dreams, split scenes, hallucinatory meetings, and hauntings: Prior meets Harper in a dream and tells her Joe is gay; Ethel Rosenberg visits Roy; Harper hallucinates "Mr. Lies," a travel agent who arranges for her to journey to Antarctica; Prior is visited by two ancestral ghosts, both also named Prior Walter; an angel greets Prior as a prophet amid a great blaze of music and lights—"God almighty ... *Very* Steven Spielberg," is Prior's response (118). In *Perestroika*, the second part of *Angels*, which was first performed in May 1991, AIDS continues to take its toll on Prior and on Roy, the angelic visitations continue as Prior learns more about his role as a prophet, and the relationship between Joe and Louis continues to drive the two, along with their confidants and their ex-lovers, to delve more deeply into the emotional and political conundrums of the age.

New York hovers significantly in the background throughout both parts of *Angels*. When Prior's friend Belize attempts to help Prior accept what may be coming to him, no matter how painful, he urges him to "Listen to the world, to how fast it goes." *They stand silently, listening, and the sounds of the city grow louder and louder, filling the stage—sounds of traffic, whistles, alarms, people, all very fast and very complex and very determinedly moving ahead.* "That's New York traffic, baby, the sound of energy, the sound of time. Even if you're hurting, it can't go back" (*Perestroika* 47–48). The New York of *Angels* is also the clichéd city of the popular imagination. "New York City. All they got there is tiny rooms," says Sister Ella Chapter to Hannah, Joe Pitt's mother, before she decides to sell her house in Utah and head east. When Joe and Louis meet at Jones Beach, facing the ocean, the stage directions call for "*The sound of waves and gulls and distant Belt Parkway traffic*," the conventions of an atmosphere called "*New York Romantic*" (*Millenium* 82 and *Perestroika* 68). Considering how varied the cast of characters is, perhaps New York is one of the few places in America surreal and miscellaneous enough to work as a setting, though the wonderful strangeness of the play might even exceed the city's capacity to give almost anything a believable context. Toward the end of *Perestroika* Hannah sits at Prior's bedside in the hospital in New York. Prior introduces her to his nurse, Emily: "Prior: This is my ex-lover's lover's Mormon mother. *(Little pause.)* Emily: Even in New York in the eighties, *that* is strange" (101).

David Dinkins presided over the city as "New York in the eighties" gave way to New York in the nineties. Dinkins had served previously as borough president of Manhattan, and his serene bearing and appeals for racial toleration during a time of escalating tension helped him win the Democratic nomination and then take the mayoral race over Rudolph Giuliani, the Republican nominee. New York had always been ethnically diverse, and the census of 1990 showed that it was getting even more so. For the first time, the city's population was less than 50 percent white. More than a quarter of New Yorkers were foreign-born. Dominicans moved into Washington Heights, Russians into Brighton Beach, Columbians into Jackson Heights and Corona, Haitians and newcomers from the Middle East into Brooklyn, and Koreans and Chinese into Queens. The "glorious mosaic," as Dinkins put it, of cultures and peoples in New York demanded a leader who could be sympathetic to the interests and concerns of an astonishingly broad array of ethnic groups.

Unfortunately for Dinkins, as for many mayors before him, city finances were hardly on the upswing as he took office. The budget deficit hampered his ability to deliver municipal services to the poor and needy he had promised to help. Jobs were lost and not replaced; arrests for drugs alone approached 100,000 per year; thousands of AIDS cases flooded the hospitals; more than 10,000 homeless people scratched out an existence on the streets. To make matters worse, the national economy was mired in a recession for much of Dinkins's single term in office, which made it difficult for the city economy to gain momentum. The mayor's performance as a soother of interethnic tensions was too uneven to compensate for the fiscal problems that troubled the city: his responses to racially inflected boycotts, shootings, and civil disturbances were frequently deemed too slow or too weak by the press, though his performance in keeping the streets peaceful during the 1992 Los Angeles riots was widely admired. The bombing by terrorists of the World Trade Center in the spring of 1993 further weakened Dinkins's chances for reelection as he faced off against Giuliani for a second time that fall.

Giuliani won the election by a slim margin, just 53,000 votes, after running a Koch-esque no-nonsense campaign that targeted Dinkins's supposed fiscal incompetence. Giuliani pared the city budget by cutting spending on education and welfare. He cultivated a good relationship with the police department that helped him to strike a blow against administrative inefficiency when he supervised the merging of the three police forces—housing, regular, and transit—into one organization in 1995. He also managed to forge something of a rapport with New York's ethnic minorities by speaking against the anti-immigrant stance of the Republican Party in spite of his affiliations with it: "You can't be a New Yorker—you can't be part of this city—and deny the contributions of immigrants," he stated in an address to the General Assembly of the United Nations in September of 1995 (qtd. in Lankevich 253). Giuliani had the good fortune to benefit from the Wall Street boom that occurred in the mid-1990s, which in turn allowed for tax cuts and budget increases which helped the upper, middle, and lower classes alike. But it was finally as an effective champion of law and order that Giuliani most impressed New Yorkers. Public safety was always a high priority for voters, but no one seemed to be able to turn around the trends that had started in the 1960s and 1970s. Due in part to monetary appropriations Dinkins had made, under Giuliani, "Peddlars, aggressive beggars, 'squeegee men' who insisted on wiping the already-clean windshields of cars stopped at lights, fare beaters on the subway, and even 'token suckers' now became targets of police action" (249). Just two years into his first term, murder, robberies, and car theft had each fallen by more than a third.

DON DELILLO

As Giuliani squared off against Ruth Messinger in the 1997 election, Don DeLillo, one of New York's most important novelists, put the finishing touches on *Underworld*, a sprawling work in which he ambitiously confronts the movements, personalities, trends, and major events of the second half of the twentieth century in America. The novel was originally inspired by a pair of headlines on the front page of *The New York Times* from October 44, 1951. DeLillo had gone to look it up out of curiosity, after having come across a story about the 40th anniversary of a memorable Dodgers-Giants baseball game that was played then. What he found was a suggestive, eerie symmetry: on one side of the front page was a headline about the game—the Giants had won the pennant on a Bobby Thompson homerun that came to be known as "the Shot Heard Round the World"—and on the other side was an announcement that the Soviets had exploded an atomic bomb, marking the onset of the Cold War. The narrative that emerged from the juxtaposition takes up a nebula of issues and tensions that surround the headlines—innocence and experience, memory and history, heroism, danger, the media, science, and violence among many others. As DeLillo traces the interconnected lives of a large and brilliantly drawn cast of characters, he takes the reader on a tour of fifty years of history. Lenny Bruce, Frank Sinatra, J. Edgar Hoover, Jackie Gleason, and Mick Jagger, among others, make appearances; historical moments are resurrected with a gripping intensity—Truman Capote's Black and White Ball, the 1965 New York blackout, the Giants' victory. The novel ranges over several settings on different continents, but much of it occurs in New York, "the womb of consciousness," where DeLillo grew up (DeLillo 623).

Donald Richard DeLillo was born on November 20, 1936, in the Bronx, where his parents, both Italian immigrants, raised him in a house near the intersection of 182nd Street and Adams Place. He attended the Cardinal Hayes High School and went on to take a communications degree at Fordham University. After graduation DeLillo worked as a copywriter for Ogilvy and Mather, an advertising agency, and rented an apartment in Murray Hill. His first short story, "The River Jordan," was published in *Epoch* magazine in 1960. Eleven years later, his first novel, *Americana,* appeared from Houghton Mifflin. His second novel, *Endzone,* was published in 1972, and *Great Jones Street*, a novel set in New York, appeared in 1973. The 1970s were a productive decade for DeLillo, and he went on to publish three more novels before the decade was out—*Ratner's Star*, *Players*, and *Running Dog*. DeLillo's novels of the 1980s only enhanced his already solid critical reputation. *The Names*, set in Europe, was followed by *White Noise*, a break-through novel for DeLillo which won him the National Book Award. His next novel, *Libra*, was a New York Times bestseller, and *Mao II*, which appeared in 1991, won the PEN/Faulkner Award for Fiction. Six years elapsed between *Mao II* and *Underworld*, DeLillo's longest and most ambitious novel, for which Scribner's paid him a one-million-dollar advance, and the publication of which was much hyped in the press.

The novel opens with a dazzling prologue that recreates the Dodgers-Giants game at the Polo Grounds on October 3, 1951. It's called "The Triumph of Death" after a Brueghel painting that is reproduced on a page of a magazine that floats into the lap of J. Edgar Hoover, who is there watching the game with Jackie Gleason, Toots Shor, and Frank Sinatra. The crowd erupts into a frenzy following Thompson's game-winning homerun. Cotter Martin, a young local fan, grabs the homerun ball and takes it home, and much of the rest of the novel is concerned with the attempts of various characters to track the ball down, verify it, own it, from Manx Martin, Cotter's father, who steals it from his son and sells it, to Nick Shay, the novel's protagonist, who comes to purchase it years later. What ensues is history, rendered collage-style as the novel jumps forward, backward, and then forward again to piece together the life and times of a huge assortment of characters whose lives are delicately linked together—by family ties, by adulterous romance, by shared aspirations, by friendship, by betrayal, sometimes by a desire for the baseball itself. For example, Manx steals the ball from Cotter and sells it to Charles Wainright who gives it to his son Chuckie; Chuckie later pilots a plane nicknamed "Long Tall Sally," a plane which resurfaces as one of the B-52s Klara Sax is painting as part of an art project; Klara Sax, it turns out, is Nick Shay's high school science teacher's ex-wife—it was with her that Nick had had an affair while he was a teenage drop-out in the early sixties. The title of the novel has a range of specific resonances, but the webs of only partly visible connections that inhabit the novel put its main meaning in evidence, which is the idiosyncratic private history that evolves outside of, or beneath, public view. Fittingly, the New York of *Underworld* is a city of intensely personal experiences and sensations:

> This was Klara Sax's summer at the roofline. She found a hidden city above the grid of fever streets. Walk and Don't Walk. Ten million bobbing heads that ride above the tideline of taxi stripes, all brain-waved differently, and yes the street abounds in idiosyncrasy, in the human veer, but you have to go to roof level to see the thing distinct, preserved in masonry and brass. She looked across the crowded sky of ventilators

and antennas and suddenly there's a quirk, some unaccountable gesture that isolates itself. Angels with butterfly wings tucked under a cornice on Bleeker Street. Or the mystery of a white clapboard cottage on the roof of an office building. Or the odd deco heads, sort of Easter Islandish, attached to the corners of a midtown tower. She found these things encouraging, dozens such that hung unauthored, with bridge cables in the distance and occasional booming skies, the false storms of summer. (371–2)

The city that Klara finds intriguing is a "hidden city" that she discovers privately, for herself, in "unaccountable" and "unauthored" things that present themselves to her. By dwelling, as Klara does here, on quirks and idiosyncrasies—the life of the city's people and objects and weather as it transpires behind the scenes and off the record—DeLillo presents a city largely free of cliché, as richly detailed as any in the literary history of the city.

Four years after *Underworld* appeared, the twin towers of the World Trade Center looming in the background of the picture on the book's dust jacket were no longer standing. Their fall was the result of a disastrous terrorist attack. On the morning of September 11, 2001—the date would come to be referred to as "9/11"—two passenger planes were hijacked and steered into the towers: an hour and a half later the stress of the planes' impact caused both buildings to collapse. Thousands of people, including the passengers of the two planes, workers who were trapped in the upper stories of the towers, bystanders on street-level, and those who came to their rescue, were killed. The attack, carried out by a terrorist group called Al Qaeda led by Osama Bin Laden, was apparently intended as a strike against the power, wealth, and way of life that the 110-story towers of the World Trade Center symbolized.

The sheer loss of human lives was devastating, as were the psychological and emotional scars left in the minds and hearts of survivors. Makeshift memorials sprang up in Union Square and elsewhere in the city; relief programs allowed people all across the country to show their support for New York and help the city heal and recover. The economic and material damages were likewise abysmal. The museums, restaurants, and stores that rely on tourism took heavy losses. Some estimates projected the number of jobs that would immediately be lost in the hundreds of thousands. Millions of feet of office space were destroyed. Nearly 300,000 tons of debris were produced by the collapse.

The many literary responses to the attacks offer a range of perspectives and span several genres. In "The Last Hours of Laódikê, Sister of Hektor," to take one example, Nicholas Christopher, a longtime New Yorker and author of several acclaimed volumes of poetry and novels, views the day of the attacks through the lens of myth. Through his uniquely spare style the action of the poem is broken into a series of suggestive images. The speaker of the poem is locked "in an icy chamber/where a torch of thorns sputters/and a man more bone than flesh/is playing music old/as time itself on a flute." There is "a girl clutching her knees" who "burns with fever before I apply/a square of moonlight to her brow." The surreal space of the "icy chamber" and the dream-like figures that haunt it are, in the last stanza of the poem, drawn into a fall like that of the twin towers: "the room falling too and the city/and no one to hear our cries/just the dead waiting in a bottomless canyon/and the sound relentless/of the gods grinding this world to dust" (Schmidt 204–5). The idea of helplessness dominates the poem, as forces beyond the speaker's control, represented here as "gods," go on "grinding this world to dust," a process whose inevitability is marked by the flute-music, "old/as time itself," which serves as accompaniment. However, the speaker's agency is not reduced to nothing, as the possibility of cooling the girl's fever by applying "a square of moonlight to her brow" suggests. Though it may not check the "falling" of the room or the city, it is nevertheless a gesture of healing, not less effectual for being overtly poetic, not less important for being unequal, by itself, to the task of diverting the "gods" from their awful work.

Mayor Giuliani, like the firemen, policemen, and other

workers who participated in the rescue effort, came to be regarded as a hero, and was named *Time* magazine's "Man of the Year." As Michael Bloomberg took over for him in 2002, New York's writers, the heroes of this book, had already begun the

New York by the Numbers

Per capital personal income for city residents in 2001: $41,289.

Total land area occupied by the city: 303 square miles.

Weight of the Statue of Liberty, in pounds: 450,000.

Miles of waterfront in New York: 578.

Number of items for sale stocked by Macy's: 500,000.

Number of ticker tape parades on Lower Broadway: 200.

Length in miles of all New York's streets combined: 6,374.6.

Number of bird species in Central Park: 215.

Year in which the first pizzeria in the United States opened in New York: 1895.

Estimated percentage of city residents living in tenements in 1901: 70.

Year in which the first ever crossword puzzle appeared, in the *New York Sun*: 1913.

Number of years the Empire State Building reigned as the world's tallest building: 42.

Number of New Yorkers who died at the Alamo in 1836: 8.

Year in which the first animated electrical sign appeared in Times Square: 1928.

Number of immigrants who entered the United States through Ellis Island from 1892–1924: 12,000,000.

Number of city-owned parks in New York: 1,701.

Average number of churches and other places of worship per square mile in New York: 11.6.

Length in feet of the Verrazano-Narrows Bridge: 4,260.

Population of New York in 2000: 8,008,278.

complex work of coming to terms with the event, replaying it at different speeds and volumes, sifting through the heap of broken images it generated. The range of idioms and perspectives and the powers of conceptualization and execution that many New York writers brought to bear on the subject of the 9/11 attacks stands as a testament to the variety and richness of the literary tradition of which they are the legatees. At their most mournful and at their most furious, at their most consoling and at their most irreverent, they assert the continuity of one of the world's most complex and important urban cultures.

THE BRONX

Home to the New York Botanical Garden and the world famous Bronx Zoo, the Bronx has a great literary heritage. Don DeLillo was born here, and F. Scott Fitzgerald once rented an apartment in the borough. The Bronx has also been a setting in famous literary works such as Nathanael West's *Miss Lonelyhearts* and Tom Wolfe's *The Bonfire of the Vanities*. The famed Yankee Stadium, featured in DeLillo's *Mao II* has been the longtime home to the Bronx Bombers.

EDGAR ALLEN POE COTTAGE

Grand Concourse and East Kingsbridge Road • 718-881-8900

Poe lived in this house between 1846 and his death in 1849, and he wrote *Ulalume* and *The Bells* here. It became a museum in 1917. The artifacts and documents are on display on Saturdays 10am–4pm, and Sundays 1am–5pm. For more information, contact the Historical Society, 3309 Bainbridge Avenue, The Bronx, NY 10467.

WAVE HILL

675 West 252 Street, Bronx, NY 10471 • 718-549-3200
www.wavehill.org

Now also home to a public garden and cultural center, Theodore Roosevelt's and Mark Twain's families once lived in the two spectacular mansions on Wave Hill grounds. Open spring/summer 9am–5:30pm, Wednesday until 9pm, closed Mondays June and July. Winter hours are Tuesday–Sunday from 9am–4:30pm, closed Mondays.

BROOKLYN

You'll find the Brooklyn Museum of Art and Brooklyn Botanical Garden in this historic borough. From Brooklyn Heights, where Walt Whitman and Truman Capote lived, to the Park Slope Historic District, Brooklyn has a wide range of literary and cultural sites to visit. Marianne Moore established her literary career in Brooklyn, and Arthur Miller was born in and based *Death of a Salesman* here. Brooklyn's neighborhoods are also a mecca of diversity, with many races and nationalities coexisting in the borough.

HART CRANE'S APARTMENT

110 Columbia Heights

Site of the apartment building Crane lived in during the 1920s while composing *The Bridge*. The New York Historical Society offers a walking tour of the Brooklyn Bridge/Brooklyn Heights neighborhood where many Hart Crane sites are featured. For more information contact Big Onion Walking Tours at 212-439-1090 or www.bigonion.com.

MANHATTAN

Poet Walt Whitman described New York City in *Leaves of Grass* as "the no more beyond of the western world." There could be no better description from a writer who called the city and its environs home. Manhattan served as a literary backdrop for centuries, from Washington Irving to Henry James, to Norman Mailer and Don DeLillo. It was the setting for the Harlem Renaissance as well as the center of the Beat Generation. It is a place of ever constant change and progress, which has fostered the growth of many intellectual and artistic movements, and will continue to do so in the future.

THE ALGONQUIN HOTEL

49 West 44th Street • 888-304-2047

The meeting place of the Round Table writers (in the Rose Room) during the 1920s. Dorothy Parker, Robert Benchley, Franklin P. Adams, Edna Ferber, and George S. Kaufman were among the Round Table's more distinguished members. They referred to themselves as the "Vicious Circle." More information is available at www.algonquinhotel.com.

AMERICAN ACADEMY OF ARTS AND LETTERS

633 West 155th Street • 212-368-5900

The honor society for American writers and artists, members of which include John Dos Passos, William Faulkner, Lillian Hellman, Henry James, Edith Wharton, Norman Mailer, Toni Morrison, and John Updike. The Academy celebrated its centennial in 1998. Hours: Thursdays–Sunday 1pm–4pm during exhibitions; closed Mondays.

BROOKLYN BRIDGE

Spans the East River joining Manhattan and Brooklyn

The Brooklyn Bridge was the world's first steel suspension bridge when it was completed in 1883. It served as an inspiration to Walt Whitman, Hart Crane, Marianne Moore, Arthur Miller and many other writers and artists.

CARPO'S CAFE

189 Bleeker Street • 212-353-2889

Carpo's was originally known as the San Remo, an Italian restaurant that became a gathering place for writers and artists such as James Baldwin, Jack Kerouac, Allen Ginsberg, William S. Burroughs, Miles Davis, Norman Mailer, Jackson Pollock, and Dylan Thomas. John Clellon Holmes wrote about San Remo in his novel *Go*, one of the first works that can be considered of the Beat Generation.

CATHEDRAL OF ST. JOHN THE DIVINE

1047 Amsterdam Avenue General Information: 212-316-7540
www.stjohndivine.org

The cornerstone of this Cathedral was laid on St. John's Day on December 27, 1892, and it is still a work in progress. The philosophy of the Cathedral—that it should serve all people—takes priority even over the completion of the massive structure. A Poets' Corner is maintained like that of Westminster Abbey. The Cathedral hours are Monday–Saturday, from 7am–6pm, Sunday 7am–7pm. To find out about tours call 212-932-7347.

CHUMLEY'S

86 Bedford Street in the West Village 212-675-4449

This is the site of one of New York's legendary literary pubs. A speakeasy during the Prohibition, Chumley's was patronized by John Dos Passos, Theodore Dreiser, F. Scott Fitzgerald, Edna St. Vincent Millay, Eugene O'Neill, Dylan Thomas, and Edmund Wilson among many other writers. Hours are 5pm–12am Sunday–Thursday; 5pm–2am Friday and Saturday.

COLUMBIA UNIVERSITY

Broadway and West 116th Street
General Information: 212-854-1754
www.columbia.edu

Founded in 1754 as King's College, Columbia University is located in the heart of Morningside Heights. Notable alums include Alexander Hamilton, Theodore Roosevelt, Zora Neale Hurston, Thomas Merton, Jack Kerouac, Allen Ginsberg, Lawrence Ferlinghetti, and Federico Garcia Lorca among many others. A visitor's center is located in room 213 of Low Library.

DELACORTE THEATER

Central Park

This is the open-air home of the New York Shakespeare Festival, which puts on two plays by the Bard each summer. Tickets are free and are distributed at the Delacorte Theater and at the Public Theater on Lafayette Street on the day of the performance. To contact the New York Shakespeare Festival call 212-539-8500.

FEDERAL HALL NATIONAL MEMORIAL

26 Wall Street • 212-825-6888
www.nps.gov/feha

Many people may not know that this is the site where George Washington took his oath of office as the country's first president. A statue commemorating the event is on display outside of the hall. It is open 9am–5pm, Monday–Friday, year-round except on national holidays.

GOTHAM BOOK MART

41 West 47th Street • 212-719-4448

Founded in 1920 by Francest Steloff, it still remains one of the hubs of New York literary activity. Famous clientele include Elizabeth Bishop, Randall Jarrell, Robert Lowell, Marianne Moore, Delmore Schwartz, Gore Vidal, Henry Miller, Allen Ginsberg, John Updike, and Tennessee Williams.

HARLEM

110th to 168th Street

What began as a Dutch settlement became the center for African-American culture in New York City over time. The Harlem Renaissance in the 1920s was a rebirth of art and literature among blacks in the community. It produced such writers as Langston Hughes and Zora Neale Hurston. Today it is home to many African-American historical sites, including the Apollo Theater and the Greater Metropolitan Baptist Church.

HORACE GREELEY STATUE

City Hall Park, on Park Row

The statue stands at what was the center of New York's bustling newspaper scene in the 19th century. Greeley's *New York Tribune, The New York World, The Recorder, The New York Daily News, The New York Press, The New York Observer, The New York Times, The Sun, The Aurora, The Literary World, The Broadway Journal,* and several other newspapers were all headquartered nearby, along Park Row and Nassau Street.

HOTEL CHELSEA

222 West 23rd Street • 212-243-3700
www.hotelchelsea.com

The Hotel Chelsea was New York's first co-operative apartment complex opening in the late 19th century. When it became a hotel in 1905, it went on to host artists, intellectuals, and writers such as William Dean Howells, Mark Twain, O. Henry, Thomas Wolfe, Mary McCarthy, Arthur Miller, Vladimir Nabokov, William S. Burroughs, and James Schuyler, among others.

INTER-CONTINENTAL THE BARCLAY NEW YORK

111 East 48th Street • 212-755-5900
http://new-york-barclay.intercontinental.com/

This hotel is formerly the site of the Barclay Hotel where Ernest Hemingway rewrote *For Whom the Bell Tolls* in four days without leaving his room. To celebrate its 75th Anniversary the hotel reclaimed its original name and is now known as Inter-Continental The Barclay.

BLUE HILL RESTAURANT

75 Washington Place • 212-539-1776

Originally known as Marta's, this was the preferred eatery of John

Dos Passos, Elinor Wylie, and William Rose Benét, among others, in the early 1920s.

MCSORLEY'S OLD ALE HOUSE

15 East 7th Street • 212-473-9148

McSorley's was founded in 1854 and remains unchanged in almost every way since opening. Surprisingly, women were not allowed admittance to the bar until 1970. Now one of the only operating saloons in New York City, it was frequented by Brendan Behan, E.E. Cummings, Amiri Baraka, Allen Ginsberg, John Lennon, Abraham Lincoln, and Frank McCourt, among others. Weekday hours are 11am–1am and on the weekends 1pm–1am.

MUSEUM OF MODERN ART

11 W. 53rd Street • 212-707-9480
www.moma.org

From its inception in 1929, the principle philosophy of MOMA has been to move beyond the narrow definition of art. It is one of the most popular attractions in mid-town Manhattan, and attracts a million and a half visitors annually. The Museum hours are Monday, 10am–5pm, Thursday–Sunday, 10am–5pm. Closed Thanksgiving Day and Christmas Day.

NATIONAL ARTS CLUB

15 Gramercy Park South • 212-475-3424
www.nationalartsclub.org

Located in the historic Tilden mansion in Gramercy Park, the National Arts Club was founded in the late 1800s by Charles de Kay. He envisioned a gathering place for members of the artistic and intellectual community. Although many events are open to members only, some exhibitions are open to the public.

NEW YORK PUBLIC LIBRARY

Fifth Avenue and 42nd Street • 212-869-8089/exhibits and events • 212-661-7220/hours
www.nypl.org

Opened in 1911 on the old Croton Reservoir site, the New York Public Library houses nearly 20 million books in a building considered among the greatest examples of Beaux-Arts architecture in the United States. It began as a consolidation of the two private libraries of John Jacob Astor and James Lenox. Closed Sundays.

NUYORICAN POETS CAFÉ

236 East 3rd Street • 212-505-8183
http://www.nuyorican.org/

Founded in 1974 to promote the culture of the Lower East Side Spanish-speaking community, the Nuyorican now hosts a variety of diverse art and literary events. It has been frequented by Lucky Cienfuegos, Sandra Maria Esteves, Amiri Baraka, Gregory Corso, Allen Ginsberg, Jimmy Santiago Baca, and Sapphire. A schedule of events is available on its website.

PIERPONT MORGAN LIBRARY

29 East 36th Street • 212-685-0610
http://www.morganlibrary.org/

Built in 1906 by J.P. Morgan to house his enormous book and art collection, the library became open to the public in 1924. In addition to three Gutenberg Bibles, it houses manuscripts by authors such as Charles Dickens and Henry David Thoreau, and music manuscripts by Bach, Mozart, and Stravinsky, among many others. It is one of the world's greatest collections of art and literature. Although the library is currently undergoing a major renovation project, it is scheduled to reopen in 2006.

PLAZA HOTEL

768 5th Ave (at 59th St.) • 212-903-3000

Originally designed as a high-rise French château by Henry Hardenbergh in 1907, the Plaza was immortalized by F. Scott Fitzgerald in *The Great Gatsby*. The ambiance is that of old New York.

PROVINCETOWN PLAYHOUSE

133 MacDougal Street
Greenwich Village

The Provincetown Playhouse opened in 1916 and launched the career of Eugene O'Neill. In close proximity to Washington Square Park, it is now home to many events of the NYU Center for Creative Performance.

SCHOMBURG CENTER FOR RESEARCH IN BLACK CULTURE

515 Malcolm X Boulevard • 212-491-2200
http://www.nypl.org/research/sc/sc.html

Opened in 1978, the Schomburg Center is one of the best centers in the world for research on African American history and culture. Richard Wright's original manuscript for *Native Son* is held among the Center's vast collection. The Schomburg Center is closed Sunday–Monday. More information about visiting hours can be found on its website.

ST. MARK'S CHURCH

131 E. 10th St.
info@poetryproject.com

Founded in 1966, the Poetry Project has featured numerous public readings by famous poets, especially the Beats, and it was the site of the only joint reading by Allen Ginsberg and Robert Lowell. St. Mark's Church continues to be a center for activism and the arts in the East Village. More information is available on www.poetryproject.com.

PLACES OF INTEREST

STATUE OF LIBERTY NATIONAL MONUMENT

Liberty Island, New York Harbor • 212-732-1236
http://www.nps.gov/stli/

Dedicated in 1886, the Statue of Liberty was a gift from the nation of France. Immigrants on their way into the United States have taken comfort in the words, "Give me your tired, your poor, your huddled masses yearning to be free," inscribed on the base of the statue. The park hours are: weekdays, 9:30am–5pm, and weekends and holidays 9:30am–5:30pm.

THE STRAND

828 Broadway • 212-473-1452
http://www.strandbooks.com/home/

The largest bookstore in the country, with nearly two million volumes in stock. Open Monday–Saturday, 9:30am–10:30pm, and on Sundays from 11am–10:30pm.

WASHINGTON IRVING STATUE

Irving Place and East 17th Street

Cast in 1885 by Friedrich Beer, the statue stood in Bryant Park before being moved in 1935 to its current location on the street developer Samuel B. Ruggles named to honor Irving.

WASHINGTON SQUARE

In the heart of Greenwich Village, the Washington Arch towers over one of the city's greatest parks. Henry James set his novel, *Washington Square*, in and around this neighborhood. Many literary figures, including Edith Wharton and John Dos Passos lived in the Washington Square area. Washington Square Park is located at 55 Washington Square South, 212-477-0351.

WEST END CAFÉ

2909 Broadway • 212-662-8830

Jack Kerouac, Allen Ginsberg, and members of the Beat Generation all frequented this bar in the 1940s. It is now an upscale jazz
club.

WHITE HORSE TAVERN

567 Hudson Street • 212-243-9260

The oldest literary bar in Greenwich Village functions as an 1880s
saloon. It has been patronized by Norman Mailer, Lawrence Ferlinghetti, Jack Kerouac, and Dylan Thomas, to whose memory a
room adjoining the bar is dedicated.

QUEENS

Queens is the largest of the five boroughs, and home to many
immigrants. Two world's fairs were held here, and the Unisphere—
the largest globe in the world—is featured in the Flushing
Meadows Corona Park area. E.L. Doctorow was born on the lower
east side. Shea Stadium is also located in Queens, and there is a
great rivalry between Yankees and Mets fans.

QUEENS MUSEUM OF ART

New York City Building
Flushing Meadows Corona Park
718-592-9700

The Queens museum displays the Panorama of New York City,
which is the world's largest architectural scale model. The
panorama covers over 9,335 square feet and is updated on a regular
basis to include all of the city's buildings. The museum is open
September–June on Wednesday–Friday from 10am–5pm, and Saturday–Sunday from 12pm–5pm. It is open July–August on
Wednesday–Sunday from 1pm–8pm.

STATEN ISLAND

A ride on the Staten Island ferry from Manhattan takes you to this quaint borough on the southern tip of the city. Staten Island is home to many unique museums, including the Staten Island Institute of Arts and Sciences, and the Staten Island Children's Museum. The borough has the most colonial-era houses in New York City.

HISTORIC RICHMOND TOWN

441 Clarke Ave. • 718-351-1611
www.historicrichmondtown.org/

Staten Island's restored rural village from the 17th century is one of its most popular tourist attractions. It contains 11 original buildings, including the 1695 Voorleezer House, which is the oldest surviving elementary school in the United States. It is open from September–June, Wednesday–Sunday from 1pm–5pm, and July–August, Wednesday–Saturday from 10am–5pm, and Sunday from 1pm–5pm.

CHRONOLOGY

1524   Giovanni da Verrazano pilots *La Dauphine* into New York harbor.

1609   Henry Hudson explores the Hudson River.

1621   Dutch West India Company chartered.

1625   Fort Amsterdam constructed.

1626   Peter Minuit purchases Manhattan from the Canarsie tribe.

1629   Patroonship program initiated to help settle the colony.

1647   Peter Stuyvesant takes over as Director-General.

1658   First hospital established in New Amsterdam.

1664   Dutch New Amsterdam becomes British New York.

1670   Publication of Daniel Denton's "A Brief Description of New York."

1673   Dutch temporarily regain rule of the city.

1674   Edmund Andros named governor.

1688   Jacob Leisler leads revolt, takes over the colony.

1689   Trinity Church dedicated.

1711   Slave market set up on Wall Street.

1712   Slaves stage major revolt.

1725   New York's first newspaper, the *New York Gazette*, established.

1729   First synagogue constructed in New York.

1732   New Theater opens.

1734   John Peter Zenger tried for libel and acquitted.

1754   King's College (Columbia University) founded.

1765   Stamp Act passed. New York merchants boycott British wares.

1767   Townshend Act passed.

1774   New York stages its own "Tea Party" in response to the Tea Act of 1773.

1776   Revolutionary War begins.

1783   British forces leave New York as the war ends. Washington Irving born.

1785   New York named capital of the United States.

1788   Society of St. Tammany convenes for the first time.

1789   George Washington inaugurated as president at Federal Hall.

1790   United States capital relocated to Philadelphia. Manhattan population: 33,131.

1792   Buttonwood Agreement unites brokers into self-regulating body that prefigures the Stock Exchange.

1798   Park Theater opens.

1804   Aaron Burr kills Alexander Hamilton in a duel.

1809   Publication of Irving's *A History of New York*.

1810   Manhattan population: 96,373.

1812   War of 1812 begins as Congress declares war on Britain.

1819   Birth of Herman Melville and Walt Whitman.

1823   New York becomes largest city in the nation. Birth of William "Boss" Tweed.

1825   DeWitt Clinton opens Erie Canal.

1827   Slavery abolished state-wide.

1829   William Cullen Bryant starts editing *New York Evening Post.*

1830   Manhattan population: 202,589.

1831   Alexis de Tocqueville visits New York.

1835   Fire ravages lower Manhattan, destroying 700 buildings.

1839   Steam packet service established between New York and Europe.

1841   Horace Greeley's *New York Tribune* begins publication.

1842   Croton Reservoir constructed. Charles Dickens visits city.

1843   Birth of Henry James.

1850   Manhattan population: 515,547.

1851   *New York Times* publishes first edition. Publication of Melville's *Moby-Dick.*

1854   Academy of Music opens.

1855   Publication of Whitman's *Leaves of Grass.*

1858   Central Park designed by Vaux and Olmstead.

1860   Abraham Lincoln addresses massive audience at Cooper Union.

1861   Civil War begins.

1862   Birth of Edith Wharton.

1863   Four-day draft riot takes place.

1870   Manhattan population: 942,292.

1871   Boss Tweed arrested. Grand Central opens.

1878   Tweed dies in prison.

1879   St. Patrick's Cathedral finished.

1880   Metropolitan Museum of Art opens. Publication of James's *Washington Square.*

1883 Brooklyn Bridge completed. Metropolitan Opera House opens.

1886 Statue of Liberty unveiled.

1888 Publication of Howells's *A Hazard of New Fortunes.*

1890 Publication of Riis's *How the Other Half Lives.* Manhattan population: 1,441,216.

1891 Carnegie Hall opens.

1893 Publication of Stephen Crane's *Maggie: A Girl of the Streets.*

1897 Waldorf-Astoria Hotel opens. Abraham Cahan helps found *The Jewish Daily Forward.*

1898 Boroughs merge to create Greater New York.

1900 Ground broken for city's first subway. Population of Greater New York: 3,437,202.

1902 Fuller Building (better known as the Flatiron Building) completed.

1903 Lyceum Theater opens.

1905 Staten Island Ferry opens. Publication of Wharton's *House of Mirth.*

1907 Publication of James's *The American Scene.*

1910 Pennsylvania Station opens.

1911 New York Public Library completed. Triangle Shirtwaist Factory fire causes 146 deaths.

1913 Apollo Theater opens in Harlem. Woolworth Building completed. Publication of Wharton's *The Custom of the Country.* Armory Show brings Modernism to America.

1915 Marianne Moore visits Alfred Stieglitz's "291" gallery. Birth of Arthur Miller.

1916 Hart Crane visits New York for the first time.

1917   United States enters World War I. Publication of
        Millay's *Renascence and Other Poems*.

1918   World War I ends.

1919   Prohibition begins with the passing of the 18th
        constitutional amendment. Yankees acquire
        Babe Ruth.

1920   Population: 5,620,048. Publication of
        Wharton's *The Age of Innocence*.

1921   Hughes publishes "The Negro Speaks of Rivers"
        in *Crisis* magazine.

1922   Publication of McKay's *Harlem Shadows* and
        Fitzgerald's *The Beautiful and the Damned*.

1923   *Time Magazine* founded.

1924   James Baldwin born.

1925   *The New Yorker* publishes its first issue. Publica-
        tion of Cullen's *Color*, Fitzgerald's *The Great-
        Gatsby*, and Dos Passos's *Manhattan Transfer*.

1926   Jimmy Walker elected mayor. Publication of
        Hughes's *The Weary Blues* and Hart Crane's
        White Buildings.

1927   Holland Tunnel opens.

1929   Stock market crashes, initiating the Great
        Depression.

1930   Chrysler Building erected.

1931   Empire State Building erected. George
        Washington Bridge opens.

1932   Jimmy Walker forced to resign.

1933   Fiorello LaGuardia elected to first of three terms
        as mayor. Publication of West's *Miss
        Lonelyhearts*.

1934   Henry Roth publishes *Call It Sleep*.

1935 First housing project in the United States constructed on Lower East Side. Clifford Odets's *Waiting for Lefty* opens at Civic Repertory Theater.

1936 Robert Moses heads the Parks Department. Birth of Don DeLillo.

1939 Rockefeller Center opens.

1940 Population: 7,454,995. Publication of Hughes's *The Big Sea*.

1941 United States enters World War II.

1945 World War II ends. La Guardia announces retirement.

1946 Headquarters for the United Nations established. George Balanchine and Lincoln Kirstei found the Ballet Society (renamed the New York City Ballet in 1948).

1947 Jackie Robinson signs with the Dodgers.

1949 Miller's *Death of a Salesman* produced.

1952 Publication of Ellison's *Invisible Man* and O'Hara's *A City Winter and Other Poems*.

1954 Robert F. Wagner begins 11-year run as mayor.

1955 Publication of Baldwin's *Notes of a Native Son*. Mailer helps found the *Village Voice*.

1956 Birth of Tony Kushner.

1959 Guggenheim Museum opens.

1960 Population: 7,781,984.

1963 Pennsylvania Station demolished.

1965 Mailer publishes *An American Dream*.

1968 200,000 students protest Vietnam War. Publication of Singer's "The Cafeteria."

1969 Publication of Bellow's *Mr. Sammler's Planet*.

1972 World Trade Center completed.

1975	City narrowly averts bankruptcy.
1977	Edward I. Koch elected mayor.
1980	Population: 7,071,639.
1985	Publication of Auster's *City of Glass* and Doctorow's *World's Fair*.
1986	Publication of Auster's *Ghosts* and *The Locked Room*.
1987	Stock market crashes. Publication of *The Bonfire of the Vanities*.
1989	David Dinkins, New York's first black mayor, elected. Publication of Hijuelos's *The Mambo Kings Sing Songs of Love*.
1990	Kushner's *Millenium Approaches* produced.
1991	Kushner's *Perestroika* produced.
1993	Rudolph Giuliani elected mayor.
1995	Publication of Ann Douglas's *Terrible Honesty: Mongrel Manhattan in the 1920s*.
1997	Publication of DeLillo's *Underworld*.
1999	Publication of *Gotham: A History of New York City to 1898* by Edwin G. Burrows and Mike Wallace.
2001	World Trade Center falls in terrorist attack.

BIBLIOGRAPHY

Alland, Alexander. *Jacob Riis: Photographer and Citizen*. New York: Aperture, 1993.

Allen, Donald, ed. *The Collected Poems of Frank O'Hara*, introduced by John Ashbery. Berkeley: University of California Press, 1995.

Allen, Frederick Lewis. *The Great Pierpont Morgan*. New York: Harper and Brothers, 1949.

Allen, Gay Wilson. *A Reader's Guide to Walt Whitman*. Syracuse: Syracuse University Press, 1970.

Allen, Oliver E. *New York, New York*. New York: Atheneum, 1990.

Asbury, Herbert. *The Gangs of New York*. New York: Thunder's Mouth Press, 2001.

Atlas, James. *Bellow: A Biography*. New York: Random House, 2000.

Auster, Paul. *The Art of Hunger: Essays, Prefaces, Interviews*. Los Angeles: Sun and Moon, 1992.

———. *The New York Trilogy: City of Glass, Ghosts, The Locked Room*. New York: Penguin, 1990.

Baldwin, James. *Collected Essays*. New York: The Library of America, 1998.

Bellow, Saul. *It All Adds Up: From the Dim Past to the Uncertain Future: A Nonfiction Collection*. New York: Viking, 1994.

———. *Mr. Sammler's Planet*. New York: Viking, 1970.

———. *Novels 1944–1953*. New York: The Library of America, 2003.

Bender, Thomas. *New York Intellect: A History of the Intellectual Life of New York City, from 1750 to the Beginnings of Our Time*. New York: Knopf, 1987.

Benfey, Christopher E. G. *The Double Life of Stephen Crane.* New York: Knopf, 1992.

Benstock, Shari. *No Gifts from Chance: A Biography of Edith Wharton.* New York: Scribners, 1994.

Birmingham, Stephen. *"Our Crowd," The Great Jewish Families of New York.* New York: Harper and Row, 1967.

Black, Mary. *Old New York in Early Photographs 1853–1901,* rev. ed. New York: Dover, 1976.

Bogen, Elizabeth. *Immigration in New York.* New York: Praeger, 1987.

Boyer, M. Christine. *Manhattan Manners: Architecture and Style 1850–1900.* New York: Rizzoli, 1985.

Burrows, Edwin G. and Mike Wallace. *Gotham: A History of New York City to 1898.* New York: Oxford University Press, 1999.

Callow, Alexander B., Jr. *The Tweed Ring.* New York: Oxford University Press, 1966.

Campbell, James. *Talking at the Gates: A Life of James Baldwin.* Boston: Faber, 1991.

Caro, Robert A. *The Power Broker: Robert Moses and the Fall of New York.* New York: Knopf, 1974.

Carr, Virginia Spencer. *Dos Passos: A Life.* Garden City: Doubleday, 1984.

Charyn, Jerome. *Metropolis: New York as Myth, Marketplace, and Magical Land.* New York: Putnam, 1986.

Cole, William, ed. *Quotable New York: A Literary Companion.* New York: Penguin, 1993.

Condon, Thomas J. *New York Beginnings: The Commercial Origins of New Netherland.* New York: New York University Press, 1968.

Connable, Alfred, and Edward Silberfarb. *Tigers of Tammany.* New York: Holt, Rinehart and Winston, 1967.

Cooper, Wayne F. *Claude McKay: Rebel Sojourner in the Harlem Renaissance.* Baton Rouge: Louisiana State University Press, 1987.

Crane, Stephen. *Maggie: A Girl of the Streets* in *The Stephen Crane Reader*, ed. R.W. Stallman. Glenview: Scott, Foresman and Co., 1972.

Crowley, John W. *The Dean of American Letters: The Late Career of William Dean Howells*. Amherst: University of Massachusetts Press, 1999.

Cuneo, Ernest. *Life with Fiorello*. New York: Macmillan, 1955.

DeLillo, Don. *Underworld*. New York: Scribners, 1997.

Denton, Daniel. *A Brief Description of New York*. London: 1670. Rpt. in *The Bulletin of the Historical Society of Pennsylvania*, vol. 1 (1845–47). Philadelphia: Merrihew and Thompson, 1848.

Dickens, Charles. *American Notes*, ed. John S. Whitley and Arnold Goldman. Harmondsworth: Penguin, 1972.

Doctorow, E.L. *World's Fair*. New York: Random House, 1985.

Dore, Ashton. *The New York School: A Cultural Reckoning*. Berkeley: University of California Press, 1992.

Dos Passos, John. *Manhattan Transfer*. Boston: Houghton Mifflin, 1925.

Douglas, Ann. *Terrible Honesty: Mongrel Manhattan in the 1920s*. New York: Farrar Straus and Giroux, 1995.

Dreiser, Theodore. *The Color of a Great City*. New York: Boni and Liveright, 1923.

———. *Sister Carrie*. Philadelphia: University of Pennsylvania Press, 1981.

Early, Gerald, ed. *My Soul's High Song: The Collected Writings of Countee Cullen, Voice of the Harlem Renaissance*. New York: Doubleday, 1991.

Edel, Leon, ed. *Henry James Letters*, vol. 4. Cambridge: Harvard University Press, 1984.

Edel, Leon. *The Life of Henry James*. Harmondsworth: Penguin, 1977.

Edmiston, Susan, and Linda D. Cirino. *Literary New York: A History and Guide*. New York: Houghton Mifflin, 1976.

Ellison, Ralph. *Invisible Man*. New York: Vintage, 1995.

Ferretti, Fred. *The Year the Big Apple Went Bust*. New York: G.P. Putnam's Sons, 1976.

Fitzgerald, F. Scott. *The Crack-Up*, ed. Edmund Wilson. New York: New Directions, 1956.

———. *The Great Gatsby*. New York: Scribner, 1995.

Fowler, Gene. *Beau James: The Life and Times of Jimmy Walker*. New York: Viking Press, 1949.

Ginsberg, Allen. *Collected Poems, 1947–1980*. New York: Harper and Row, 1984.

Gooch, Brad. *City Poet: The Life and Times of Frank O'Hara*. New York: Knopf, 1993.

Graham, Stephen. *New York Nights*. New York: Doran, 1927.

Green, Martin. *New York 1913: The Armory Show and the Paterson Strike Pageant*. New York: Scribner's, 1988.

Guilbaut, Serge. *How New York Stole the Idea of Modern Art: Abstract Expressionism, Freedom, and the Cold War*. trans. Arthur Goldhammer. Chicago: University of Chicago Press, 1983.

Hadda Janet. *Isaac Bashevis Singer: A Life*. New York: Oxford University Press, 1997.

Hall, Donald, ed. *The Oxford Book of American Literary Anecdotes*. New York: Oxford University Press, 1981.

Hammer, Langdon. *O My Land, My Friends: The Selected Letters of Hart Crane*. New York: Four Walls Eight Windows, 1997.

Hapgood, Hutchins. *The Spirit of the Ghetto*. Funk and Wagnalls, 1902.

Hijuelos, Oscar. *The Mambo Kings Sing Songs of Love*. New York: Farrar Straus and Giroux, 1989.

Hone, Philip. *The Diary of Philip Hone, 1828–1851*. ed. Allan Nevins. New York: Dodd, Mead and Co., 1936.

Howe, Irving. *World of Our Fathers*. New York: Simon and Schuster, 1976.

Howells, Mildred, ed. *Life in Letters of William Dean Howells*, vol. 1. New York: Doubleday, Doran and Company, 1928.

Howells, William Dean. *A Hazard of New Fortunes*, introduced by Tony Tanner. New York: Oxford University Press, 1990.

Huggins, Nathan Irvin, ed. *Voices from the Harlem Renaissance*. New York: Oxford University Press, 1976.

Hughes, Langston. *Selected Poems of Langston Hughes*. New York: Vintage Classics, 1990.

Innes, John. H. *New Amsterdam and Its People*. New York: Charles Scribner's Sons, 1902.

Irving, Washington. *History, Tales and Sketches*. New York: The Library of America, 1983.

James, Henry. *The American Scene*, introduced by Irving Howe. New York: Horizon Press, 1967.

————. *Washington Square*, introduced by Louis S. Auchincloss. New York: Heritage Press, 1971.

Jameson, J. Franklin, ed. *Narratives of New Netherland, 1609–1664*. New York: Charles Scribner's Sons, 1909.

Johnston, Johanna. *The Heart That Would Not Hold: A Biography of Washington Irving*. New York: Evans, 1971.

Kaplan, Justin. *Walt Whitman: A Life*. New York: Simon and Schuster, 1980.

Kasinitz, Philip. *Caribbean New York: Black Immigrants and the Politics of Race*. Ithaca: Cornell University Press, 1992.

Kenney, Alice P. *Stubborn for Liberty: The Dutch in New York*. Syracuse: Syracuse University Press, 1975.

Kessler, Henry H., and Eugene Rachlis. *Peter Stuyvesant and His New York*. New York: Random House, 1959.

Kushner, Tony. *Angels in America: A Gay Fantasia on National Themes*. New York: Theatre Communications Group, 1993.

Lankevich, George J. *American Metropolis: A History of New York City*. New York: New York University Press, 1998.

Lee, Basil. *Discontent in New York City, 1861–1865*. Washington, D.C.: Catholic University of America Press, 1943.

Lehman, David. *The Last Avant-Garde: The Making of the New York School of Poets.* New York: Doubleday, 1998.

Lewis, David L. *The Portable Harlem Renaissance Reader.* New York: Penguin, 1995.

Lingeman, Richard R. *Theodore Dreiser: An American Journey.* New York: J. Wiley and Sons, 1993.

Lopate, Phillip, ed. *Writing New York: A Literary Anthology.* New York: Library of America, 1998.

Lyman, Susan E. *The Story of New York.* New York: Crown, 1964.

Mailer, Norman. *An American Dream.* New York: The Dial Press, 1965.

Mariani, Paul L. *The Broken Tower: A Life of Hart Crane.* New York: W. W. Norton, 1999.

Martin, Jay. *Nathanael West: The Art of His Life.* New York: Farrar, Straus and Giroux, 1970.

Mabbott, Thomas Olive, ed. *Doings of Gotham.* Pottsville: Jacob E. Spannuth, 1929.

McClatchy, J. D., ed. *Edna St. Vincent Millay: Selected Poems.* New York: The Library of America, 2003.

McKay, Claude. *Selected Poems of Claude McKay.* New York: Harcourt, Brace, 1953.

McLaren, Joseph, ed. *The Collected Works of Langston Hughes*, vol. 13. Columbia: University of Missouri Press, 2002.

Meade, Marion. *Dorothy Parker: What Fresh Hell Is This?* New York: Villard, 1988.

Melville, Herman. "Bartleby, the Scrivener" in *Billy Budd and Other Tales.* New York: New American Library, 1961.

———. *Moby-Dick or The Whale.* New York: Oxford University Press, 1947.

———. *Pierre Or, The Ambiguities*, ed. Henry A. Murray. New York: Hendricks House, 1949.

Ment, David. *The Shaping of a City: A Brief History of Brooklyn.* New York: Brooklyn Educational and Cultural Alliance, 1979.

Meyers, Jeffrey. *Scott Fitzgerald: A Biography*. New York: Harper-Collins, 1994.

Milford, Nancy. *Savage Beauty: A Life of Edna St. Vincent Millay*. New York: Random House, 2001.

Miller, Arthur. *Death of a Salesman*. New York: Viking, 1949.

———. *Timebends: A Life*. New York: Grove Press, 1987.

Mills, Hilary. *Mailer: A Biography*. New York: Empire Books, 1982.

Molesworth, Charles. *Marianne Moore: A Literary Life*. New York: Atheneum, 1990.

Moore, Marianne. *The Complete Poems of Marianne Moore*. New York: Viking, 1967.

———. *A Marianne Moore Reader*. New York: Viking, 1961.

Morris, Christopher D., ed. *Conversations with E. L. Doctorow*. Jackson: University Press of Mississippi, 1999.

Murphy, Henry C., ed. *Anthology of New Netherland*. New York: Bradford Club, 1865.

Myers, Andrew B., ed. *The Knickerbocker Tradition: Washington Irving's New York*. Tarrytown: Sleepy Hollow Restorations, 1974.

Osofsky, Gilbert. *Harlem: The Making of a Ghetto*. New York: Harper and Row, 1966.

Parker, Hershel. *Herman Melville: A Biography*. Baltimore: Johns Hopkins University Press, 1996.

Rampersad, Arnold. *The Life of Langston Hughes*. New York: Oxford University Press, 2002.

Riis, Jacob A. *How the Other Half Lives*, introduced by Donald N. Bigelow. New York: Hill and Wang, 1957.

Sawyers, June Skinner. *The Greenwich Village Reader: Fiction, Poetry, and Reminiscences*. New York: Cooper Square Press, 2001.

Schmidt, Elizabeth, ed. *Poems of New York*. New York: Knopf, 2002.

Schumacher, Michael. *Dharma Lion: A Biography of Allen Ginsberg*. New York: St. Martins, 1992.

Simon, Marc, ed. *Complete Poems of Hart Crane*, introduced by Harold Bloom. New York: Liveright, 1986.

Singer, Isaac Bashevis. *The Collected Stories of Isaac Bashevis Singer*. New York: Farrar Straus and Giroux, 1982.

Stoddard, Lothrop. *Master of Manhattan: The Life of Richard Croker*. New York: Longmans, Green and Co., 1931.

Strong, George Templeton. *The Diary of George Templeton Strong: The Civil War, 1860–1865*, ed. Allan Nevins and Milton Halsey Thomas. New York: Macmillan, 1952.

de Tocqueville, Alexis. *Democracy in America*, vol. 2, ed. Phillips Bradley. New York: Knopf, 1946.

Tomkins, Calvin. *Merchants and Masterpieces: The Story of the Metropolitan Museum*, rev. ed. New York: Henry Holt, 1989.

Ward, Geoff. *Statutes of Liberty: The New York School of Poets*. New York: St. Martin's, 1993.

Watson, Steven. *Strange Bedfellows: The First American Avant-Garde*. New York: Abbeville Press, 1991.

———. *The Harlem Renaissance: Hub of African-American Culture, 1920–1930*. New York: Pantheon, 1995.

West, Nathanael. *Miss Lonelyhearts and The Day of the Locust*. New York: Modern Library, 1998.

Wharton, Edith. *The Age of Innocence*. New York: Random House, 1943.

———. *The Custom of the Country*. New York: Charles Scribner's Sons, 1913.

———. *The House of Mirth*. New York: Charles Scribner's Sons, 1905.

Whitehead, Colson. *The Colossus of New York: A City in 13 Parts*. New York: Doubleday, 2003.

Whitman, Walt. *Complete Poetry and Collected Prose*, ed. Justin Kaplan. New York: The Library of America, 1982.

Wilson, Sondra Kathryn, ed. *The* Crisis *Reader: Stories, Poetry, and*

Essays from the NAACP's Crisis *Magazine*. New York: Random House, 1999.

WPA Writers Program. *A Maritime History of New York*. Garden City: Doubleday, Doran, 1941.

Wolfe, Tom. *The Bonfire of the Vanities*. New York: Farrar Straus and Giroux, 1990.

WEBSITES

100 Years of New York City
www.nytimes.com/specials/nyc100

212.net – New York City Trivia
www.212.net/trivia.htm

NYC & Company: New York City's Official Tourism Web Site
www.nycvisit.com

New York Fast Facts and Trivia
www.50states.com/facts/newyork.htm

New York, N.Y.
www.infoplease.com/ipa/A0108570.html

FURTHER READING

Anbinder, Tyler. *Five Points: The 19th Century New York City Neighborhood That Invented Tap Dance, Stole Elections, and Became the World's Most Notorious Slum.* New York: Plume, 2002.

Charyn, Jerome. *Metropolis: New York as Myth, Marketplace, and Magical Land.* New York: Putnam, 1986.

Cole, William, ed. *Quotable New York: A Literary Companion.* New York: Penguin, 1993.

Dore, Ashton. *The New York School: A Cultural Reckoning.* Berkeley: University of California Press, 1992.

Edmiston, Susan, and Linda D. Cirino. *Literary New York: A History and Guide.* New York: Houghton Mifflin, 1976.

Feirstein, Sanna. *Naming New York: Manhattan Places and How They Got Their Names.* New York: New York University Press, 2001.

Hall, Donald, ed. *The Oxford Book of American Literary Anecdotes.* New York: Oxford University Press, 1981.

Homberger, Eric. *The Historical Atlas of New York City.* New York: Henry Holt, 1998.

Jackson, Kenneth T., ed. *The Encyclopedia of New York City.* New Haven: Yale University Press, 1995.

———, and David S. Dunbar, eds. *Empire City: New York Through the Centuries.* New York: Columbia University Press, 2002.

Lankevich, George J. *American Metropolis: A History of New York City.* New York: New York University Press, 1998.

Lopate, Phillip, ed. *Writing New York: A Literary Anthology.* New York: Library of America, 1998.

Ment, David. *The Shaping of a City: A Brief History of Brooklyn.* New York: Brooklyn Educational and Cultural Alliance, 1979.

Riis, Jacob A. *How the Other Half Lives*, introduced by Donald N. Bigelow. New York: Hill and Wang, 1957.

Schmidt, Elizabeth, ed. *Poems of New York*. New York: Knopf, 2002.

Ward, Geoff. *Statutes of Liberty: The New York School of Poets*. New York: St. Martin's, 1993.

Watson, Steven. *Strange Bedfellows: The First American Avant-Garde*. New York: Abbeville Press, 1991.

———. *The Harlem Renaissance: Hub of African-American Culture, 1920–1930*. New York: Pantheon, 1995.

Whitehead, Colson. *The Colossus of New York: A City in 13 Parts*. New York: Doubleday, 2003.

WEBSITES

100 Years of New York City
www.nytimes.com/specials/nyc100

Museum of the City of New York
www.mcny.org

New York City
www.nyc.com

New York City and Company–New York City's Official Tourism Web Site
www.nycvisit.com

New York City Government Home Page
www.nyc.gov

New York Fast Facts and Trivia
www.50states.com/facts/newyork.htm

INDEX

PICTURE **CREDITS**

CONTRIBUTORS

HAROLD BLOOM is Sterling Professor of the Humanities at Yale University. He is the author of over 20 books, including *Shelley's Mythmaking* (1959), *The Visionary Company* (1961), *Blake's Apocalypse* (1963), *Yeats* (1970), *A Map of Misreading* (1975), *Kabbalah and Criticism* (1975), *Agon: Toward a Theory of Revisionism* (1982), *The American Religion* (1992), *The Western Canon* (1994), and *Omens of Millennium: The Gnosis of Angels, Dreams, and Resurrection* (1996). *The Anxiety of Influence* (1973) sets forth Professor Bloom's provocative theory of the literary relationships between the great writers and their predecessors. His most recent books include *Shakespeare: The Invention of the Human* (1998), a 1998 National Book Award finalist, *How to Read and Why* (2000), *Genius: A Mosaic of One Hundred Exemplary Creative Minds* (2002), and *Hamlet: Poem Unlimited* (2003). In 1999, Professor Bloom received the prestigious American Academy of Arts and Letters Gold Medal for Criticism, and in 2002 he received the Catalonia International Prize.

JESSE ZUBA is a poet and freelance writer who has studied literature at both Princeton University and Yale University. In addition to his poetry and this volume on New York, he has written on Elizabeth Bishop.